Bournillon cliffs in the Bourne gorge.

Roc Cornafion (2049m) seen from SW, Roybon hut (1450m).

VERCORS-DÉVOLUY

MOUNTAINS AND LANDSCAPES

mountain walking and touring guide

Michael Peyron

West Col

VERCORS-DÉVOLUY MOUNTAINS AND LANDSCAPES

First published in the United Kingdom by
West Col Productions
Goring Reading Berks. RG8 9AA

Copyright © 1994 Michael Peyron

Printed and made in England

SBN 906227 55 0

Acknowledgements

Various companions, self-categorised as the A and B teams, have accompanied me during the past 3 years in covering the ground for this guide. My wife Josiane apart, who has joined me for many of the expeditions, and resisting the identification of teams, the main activists to whom I am in debt for much assistance are: G Espagnac, A Jourdan, E and M Hatt, B Pedroletti, B Quenot, G and S Spilliaert, G and M Waeckel, and the peripatetic P and R Collomb.

Michael Peyron Grenoble February 1994

Contents

Grand Ferrand from Col de la Croix (SW).

Illustrations

All uncredited illustrations are from the Peyron archive.

Maps

Summit of Gargas.

ABBREVIATIONS

c	circa (approximately)
CAF	French Alpine Club
DR	Didier & Richard (maps and guides)
E	east
GR	grande randonnée (long distance path/trek)
GTA	Grande Traversée des Alpes moyenne montagne
h	hour(s)
IGN	French national mapping agency
km	kilometres
L	left (direction)
m	metre(s)
min	minutes
M du P	maison du parc (office or hut)
N	north
PNV	Parc naturel régional du Vercors
pt.	point (spot height)
R	right (direction)
S	south
VTT	mountain bike(ing)
W	west
4WD	4-wheel drive (vehicle)

Intermediate compass directions are indicated: SW, NE, etc.

Telephone numbers are given in blocks of 4 x 2 digits = 8 figures.

Technical rock climbing grades commence with I and rise to VII; each grade may be qualified with plus (+) or minus (-) signs, indicating high or low in grade.

GENERAL MAP

Isère

GRENOBLE

Lans-en-V

Villard-de-Lans

Vizille

Bourne

I S È R E

△ 2284

△ 2390 La Matheysine

La Chapelle-en-V

V e r c o r s

△ 2341

Léoncel

Chabeuil

1706

Vassieux

△ 2208

1769 △ **La Mure**

Isère

VALENCE

Rhône

T r i è v e s

Corps

Mens

D e v o l u y

Drôme

Champsaur

2789 △

Die

D i o i s

Crest

Drôme

Châtillon-en-Diois

2051 △

Agnières

St-Étienne-en-D.

△ 1589

D R Ô M E

Luc-en-Diois

Lus-la-Croix-Haute

H A U T E S

2709 △

B o c h a i n e

La Roche des A.

Dieulefit

△ 1606

La Motte C.

Valdrôme

Aspres-sur-Buëch

Veynes

A L P

△ 1338

1757 △

Aspremont

N y o n s a i s

Rémuzat

Serres

B

Valréas

Nyons

Eygues

N face of Grande Moucherolle.

Introduction

This work began life as a comprehensive account of the mountain landscapes of Provence. Since 1991 it has become expanded – due to ever-widening peregrinations of the author and his helpers – to include large tracts of the French Pre-Alps, right up to Grenoble. Thus this first volume contains areas known as the Vercors, Trièves, Matheysine, Diois, Bochaine, Dévoluy and Gapençais. The second volume, to follow, will include nearly the whole of Provence in numerous regional groups.

Not content with describing the best walks and climbs to attractive summits, both works provide information and comment of a general nature about the inhabitants of each district, economic matters, characteristics of the terrain and topography, natural history and folklore; public services, accommodation, etc.

Most of the pedestrian routes selected are suitable for all comers of all ages; everyone should be kitted out in mountain clothing and boots (see Equipment, below). Experienced mountain walkers and scramblers should encounter no difficulties. In a few locations route finding might be a problem, and in fewer still technical scrambling/rock climbing may be necessary. Which is which is clearly stated.

Access International airport at Lyon-Satolas; frequent daily flights from the UK and elsewhere; fly-drive schemes. Onward bus service to Grenoble (1h15) and other destinations. Cheapest hotel near airport is Formule 1, on S side of the N6, about 3.5km before (SE of) the junction/turning for airport which lies some distance to the N. Grenoble has a domestic airport at St-Etienne de St-Geoirs, S of the N85 between the city (30 min away) and Satolas. Twice weekly charter flights from the UK in winter (for skiers) and for a shorter time in summer.

Public transport French Railways (SNCF) operate regular daily services from Grenoble, S to Veynes, stopping at Monestier-de-Clermont and Lus-la-Croix-Haute. There are similar services Valence to Die and onward to Veynes and Gap.

Grenoble itself is served daily from London (Victoria Coach Terminal) by an all-night bus. Grenoble coach terminal is right next door to the railway station.

Operating out of Grenoble the main bus companies are VFD, SCAL and 'Les Cars du Vercors'. Grenoble-Gap is served twice a day by VFD and SCAL. Intermediate points such as Corps and La Mure have respectively 4 and 5 services daily; La Mure may also be reached in summer by a combination of road and rail, thanks to VFD and La Mure railway. Longer distance, 2 services daily by VFD and SCAL, Grenoble-Sisteron has stops at Monestier, Clelles, Lus, St-Julien, Aspres and Serres.

Locally, Grenoble-Vercors, 4 daily rotations to Villard-de-Lans by VFD, with additional services by 'Les Cars du Vercors' (based in Villard). In Dévoluy, Cars Arnaud handle traffic between Veynes and Superdévoluy. In Drôme, Rapides Verts run a shuttle between Die railway station and Châtillon.

Where all these services pass through villages described in the guide, a bus service is so noted.

Equipment   In spring and summer, while training shoes or similar could be adequate for many excursions, mountain walking boots are recommended for comfort and safety. Similarly long trousers and shirts with sleeves. Carry alternatives such as shorts; otherwise thistle, brambles, nettles and rough stony ground may cause discomfort. Even on warm days a windjacket should be taken, and a waterproof for days of doubtful weather. Other essentials are a water bottle, snack foods, suntan lotion, dark glasses and headgear for sun protection; also a simple first aid kit. A stick or ski pole is handy for steep ascents/descents or for warding off sheep dogs. The latter are not a serious problem as in other parts of upland Europe, eg. Spain and Greece. All necessary bits should fit conveniently into a daysack.

Emulating backpackers loads and working laboriously along GR routes is a situation rigorously avoided in this work. A few tours on ski are included for those so tempted and so equipped.

General behaviour   Dogs must be kept on a lead. Many areas coincide with alpine pastures (June-September) and visitors are expected to cause minimum disturbance to pastoral life. In most upland places 4WD vehicles and trail bikes are strictly forbidden; elsewhere even access for mountain bikes is regulated. To avoid unpleasant surprises apply for information at the nearest Syndicat d'Initiative (tourist office); there are many notice boards and signposts stating local regulations. Close all gates, respect property and bring your litter back to a roadside bin.

Maps   The following are widely available from any good stock holder, including West Col, in Western Europe. Note that IGN 1:50,000 Orange statutory series (not listed) has been generally withdrawn from public sale and are difficult to obtain.

IGN 1:250,000 Red series	#112 Savoie-Dauphiné
	Overall planning
Michelin 1:200,000	# 77 Valence/Grenoble/Gap
motoring/road maps	# 81 Montélimar/Avignon/Digne
IGN 1:100,000 Green series	# 54 Grenoble/Gap
	Best planning map
	# 60 Cavaillon/Digne les Bains
DR 1:50,000	# 5 Diois-Baronnies
# 7 Gapençais	# 12 Vercors
# 38 Grenoble Sud	*unfortunate variable quality*
general route planning	*sheets overlap*
IGN 1:50,000 Park series	#305 Vercors
IGN TOP25 1:25,000	#3136 ET Combe Laval/Lente
detailed route maps	#3138 OT Motte/Chalançon
#3235 OT Autrans	#3236 OT Villard-de-Lans
#3237 OT Glandasse	#3336 OT La Mure/Valbonnais
#3336 ET Les Deux Alpes	#3337 OT Dévoluy/Obiou
#3338 ET Gap	#3437 OT Champsaur

Accommodation   In each area particulars are given for moderately priced hotels, including roadside inns/restaurants, gîtes d'étape and (when they exist) mountain huts. The cheapest restaurant meal, usually described as *plat du jour* (one meat and vegetable course) averaged 55Fr in 1993; however, a large helping of fish and chips might be had for 30Fr. A room for 2 with self-contained bathroom suite in a one star hotel, 180Fr. Well equipped campsite, tent and vehicle, 2 people, 30-40 Fr. Mountain huts are roughly the same cost as campsites.

Weather   Throughout Europe traditional fine spells that once could be relied on for specific regions have been severely disrupted (often attributed to the 'greenhouse' effect), so that many visits have been spoiled by rain and even snow. For instance, in 1991 and 1992 especially poor weather dominated all the region in early and late summer. Moreover, a sort of freak spring in mid-winter has occurred, producing crisp, fine conditions at altitude and fog in low-lying areas - ideal for walking between the 1500-2000m level but detrimental to skiing at various resorts. Thus given the onset of totally unpredictable nature of local weather patterns, visitors should bring a variety of garments adapted to changing conditions. Normally in high summer (July-August) the heat can be intense, roads are busy and many parties are about. Several hot days often culminate in afternoon thunderstorms, relenting at dusk and bringing cooler air and clear blue skies next day in their wake. June and September are traditionally more satisfactory - ignoring the contradictory weather patterns noted above. Winter months are very tricky and often dangerous and visitors are warned against venturing on routes described hereafter except at elevations below 1400m. Despite the unrelieved monotony of its plateau, the Vercors in poor conditions and bad visibility should not be under-estimated. There are numerous unexpected holes to fall into, slippery grass slopes and treacherous rockbands. The disappearance of careless hikers has been frequently reported over the past decade. Then it goes without saying that map and compass are essential.

Road network   S of Grenoble the N75 and N85 are perfectly adequate during weekdays, similarly lesser roads in the Vercors. But they all feature an abundance of swervery and limited opportunity for overtaking; so at weekends and holidays traffic seizes up rapidly. (The on-going debate for a Grenoble to Gap motorway has a strong environmental lobby in opposition).

There is little room for mistakes on these roads and vehicles must be in good fettle, especially when descending the notorious Laffrey hill. Secondary roads see little congestion; some single track ones need care when passing a vehicle coming in the opposite direction. Even the most minor roads have a good surface at present. Any particular failing in this respect will be noted in descriptions; also the nature of unsurfaced piste tracks used for gaining access or altitude, and parking places.

Road warriors   This title was awarded to French motorists by a prominent American weekly a few years back. The truth is that there does seem to be a higher percentage of aggressive drivers in France than in any other European country. Foreign visitors should accordingly remain cautious, courteous, discreet and unflappable in a chance encounter with one of these rogue motorists. Slow down and let him pass. Beware especially Saturday evenings when all the show-offs indulge in illegal drink-and-drive 'contests', usually among local youths trying to impress girl friends.

Theft from cars   While a common problem today all over Western Europe, some areas are relatively free from this scourge. We have not encountered or had a report about a single theft within the area of this guide over a period of 3 years. (However, almost an opposite situation is due to be revealed in the second volume of this work on Provence). For security (and insurance rules), do not leave articles visible inside a locked vehicle; put them away in the boot.

Mountain biking   *V T T* (*vélo tout-terrain*) is now the best known and most typical of new-fangled activities that mountain resorts with insufficient snow and long summers have had to encourage.

16

Bikes can be hired almost everywhere. Frenchmen adopting this 'sport' are probably more single-minded than most. They are little given to amateurism and dedication is intense, putting their *heures de loisir* to maximum use. Enthusiastic visitors can arrange to be taken in bike-carrying vehicles to scenic starting points and collected the same way at another finish. Most of this activity is done at present in the Vercors.

Other activities   Rock climbing began in the Vercors long before widespread mountain walking and backpacking. The Obiou, king of Dévoluy, has technical routes dating back 75 years while Mont Aiguille (grade III in pristine condition) was climbed 500 years ago.

Recent youthful 'crazy' sports include river-running or gorge-scrambling (in French, *le canyoning*), a blend of canoeing and potholing much pursued in Vercors and Diois, and para-gliding. The latter, being a fairly cheap and convenient form of solo flying, has taken over from its more complex relative, hang-gliding, with local tuition available in some resorts. These activities remain for the specialist enthusiast and tourists should refrain from participation.

Road safety sign.

Historical events

218 BC Hannibal crosses Alps. While actual route is hotly contested by scholars, Die claims this honour. The RN93 is loudly publicised as Hannibal's Road, with the Drôme and Bez valleys leading onto Trièves as the most likely itinerary.

69 BC Former Vocontian capital Lucus Augusti (Luc-en-Diois) is sacked and replaced by Dea Augusta (Die) as the provincial capital.

58 BC Julius Caesar is supposed to have passed through Dévoluy.

AD 379 Roman emperor Gratian grants Cularo (Grenoble) 'civitas' status, hence the later name 'Gratianopolis', from which the modern name is derived.

412-992 Barbarian invasions. In turn many occupied the area and left - Visigoths (412), Burgundians, Lombards (574), Franks and Saracens (over centuries), Hungarians (921).

992-1552 Saracens finally expelled. Feudal rule with the Dauphins as sovereign lords descends on the region. Life is characterised by grinding poverty, paternalism, bigotry, superstition and mistrust of outsiders. This lasts till the French Revolution in 1789. The Dauphin family crest was a dolphin. They owned castles at Grenoble, Vizille and La Mure, where their wives usually resided, while the men and other lordly figures played war-games among themselves.

Religious orders of various denominations such as Templars and Cistercians thrived in the area and generally attempted to alleviate the sufferings of the serfs.

Gradually the French kings draw the alpine regions into their orbit - the Dauphiné in 1349, Provence in 1481. From here they could hunt deer in the vast forests and wage war on their enemies in Italy. In June 1492, Charles VIII was apparently angered that inaccessible Mont Aiguille should be the one fortress in his kingdom never to have been trampled by his victorious armies. He immediately dispatched one of his knights, Dom Julien of Montélimar, with a fully equipped assault party to vanquish the offending peak. Thus was born the popular sport of alpinism - so the French Alpine Club claims (not correct, of course!).

1552-1626 Eight religious wars between Protestants (Huguenots) and Catholics are brutal and, in the end, largely indecisive.

During this period the great Protestant captain Lesdiguières, who dominated the holy fight, captured Grenoble in 1590, against the trend of events. But despite this success and considerable new fortifications the city was soon lost again.

1626-1789   Outbreaks of religious unrest lead to crushing all protestant worship and absolutist rule by order of Louis XIV. In wars between France and Savoy (now Italy), the area is invaded and in time freed again. On each occasion an army descends on a particular district, troops are billeted in local houses which imposes a great burden on the population. Food and pack animals are commandeered in such quantities that the poor are reduced to eating bread, chestnuts and sometimes bark and grass. The only animals left are ailing nags and worn-out donkeys - even these are eventually seized.

In 1787 Protestants receive tardy legal recognition. Local ferment among the peasantry causes disturbances in Grenoble and Vizille in 1788. The long impending *jacquerie* finally occurs in Dévoluy when Mâlemort Castle is destroyed by local villeins, while in the Vercors the rabble sack Léoncel Abbey. Wolves and bears still roam forests at the time of the Revolution, and journeymen could fall off rickety ladders and handrails in gorges and across cliffs. Footpaths and mule paths were hazardous and dangerous, especially after dark. Wretchedly poor peasants plying menial trades or practising timber-rustling run the gauntlet of beast, game keeper and landowner.

1789 to date   Napoleonic wars maintain an illusion of an imminent Golden Age. Many young men from the region give their lives for the Emperor, who remains a compellingly popular figure. True freedom and relative prosperity are not to come for nearly a century.

On return from exile in Elba in 1815, Napoleon's march from the Riviera is an unbroken chain of success. Sub-prefects, colonels and generals either flee at his approach or rally to his standard. After occupying Castellane, Digne and Sisteron, Gap and La Mure welcome him readily enough. But at Laffrey, on the N rim of the Matheysine lakes plateau, a regiment of Foot block the way, ready to open fire. In a now-famous episode Napoleon boldly faces them single-handed and soon wins them over to his cause. After this there is no further resistance and Vizille then Grenoble, the big local garrison town, are occupied without more ado.

Living conditions continue to stagnate and failed harvests cause intense hardship to the severely exploited peasantry. The military clamp-down leads to full-scale insurrection late in 1851. The insurgents retreat, are hunted down and the movement is ruthlessly suppressed. Accordingly, in the 1850s a large contingent emigrates from the miserable rural areas. Railways linking key population centres to outlying districts are opened from 1878. With better communications, education programmes and improving the quality of life become priorities. Yet roads remain unmade and bad well into the 20th century.

After 1910 another wave of rural emigration chiefly heads south towards coastal areas – the *bon pays* – away from the cold, inhospitable mountains. Many of these emigrants from the Gapençais, Bochaine and Dévoluy maintain ties with their land of origin, down to the present day, with later generations either moving back permanently, or to set up secondary residences. Only tourism after 1960 has reversed the trend of centuries.

The fashion for touring, in its initial alpine scrambling and mountaineering phase, introduced by Victorian gentlemen like WAB Coolidge, himself a visitor to Vercors and Dévoluy in 1881 and 1888, and one of the great explorers over many years of the neighbouring High Dauphiné Alps, is slow to develop. Until World War 2 touring and climbing were more or less the exclusive preserve of the small mountaineering fraternity whose members generally resorted to the services of local chamois-poachers doubling as guides, although the English began making guideless ascents in the Dauphiné in the 1870s. Even Vercors, despite proximity to Grenoble, was comparatively unfrequented and little known to the outside world, with the exception of its NE tip at St-Nizier and Lans-en-Vercors.

After the 1944 rising, the Vercors plateau and its martyred population became national institutions and, very soon, a living legend. A knock-on effect of this was that, in the post-war period hotel-based tourism underwent a first phase of development which gradually extended to the whole area. Then in the 1960s a new myth was born with the appearance of the *or blanc* phenomenon (white gold), as ski resorts mushroomed on alpine slopes. Several sites in Vercors and the self-styled 'integrated' location at Super-Dévoluy (1966-67) underwent similar dramatic transformation, with the Grenoble Winter Olympics (1968) giving added impetus. Parallel with this development of downhill skiing came a surge in cross-country skiing, for which the Vercors was to become famous. All these tourist-related activities created fresh jobs and produced a slowdown in emigration.

Eventually, as an increasingly materialistic, TV-watching consumer society turned to outdoor games as its new religion, a further

20

series was added to the list: archery, backpacking, bridge (bungy) jumping *(saut à l'élastique)*, fishing, equestrian treks of all kinds, hunting, mountain biking, specialised rock climbing and para-gliding, for all of which there is ample scope throughout the Dauphiné Pré-alps.

This diversification has proved its worth in a socio-economic context recently rocked by a dry cycle in winter that had several resorts teetering on the brink. Villard-de-Lans and Gresse-en - Vercors hardly had any snow for 3 successive years, with dire results for the latter. Piste-skiing en masse has thus proved to be something of a white elephant.

Despite these vicissitudes, nowadays tourism is arguably the biggest cash-earner for much of the rural population, although the seasonal nature is a frequent source of headaches for those who yearn for some measure of job security. While foreign markets remain targeted (numerous British tour operators go into this region), local resorts, hotels and gîtes d'étape keep going thanks to a huge urban reservoir of potential country-goers, chiefly in Grenoble but also in Gap and Die, not to mention Lyon. Even weekenders from as far away as Marseille make incursions to the Gapençais, Dévoluy and Bochaîne.

THE 1944 VERCORS RISING

Tragic events account for the undying fame of the area and its heroic defenders which led to the rapid collapse of the German army in SE France. A massive post-war cover-up left many details shrouded in ambiguity, and it is only recently that a coherent picture of the operation has emerged. There have been reputations to protect, including De Gaulle's - seen by historians as indirectly responsible for the Vercors disaster.

Most of the *franc-tireurs* groups of camps set up on the plateau in 1942-43 had already been broken up by Italian troops. But more *maquisards* converged on Vercors throughout 1943 until there was an impressive build-up. It was a miscellaneous assortment of regular French army officers and NCOs, many of them former members of the Grenoble garrison. The rank and file consisted largely of pro-Gaullist and pro-Anglo-American resistance fighters, who were joined at the last moment by a large number of untrained civilians. After initial friction between the military and civilian element, Colonel Huet and Chavant, acting as 'prefect of Vercors', welded the whole into a close-knit group.

When it came to the fight, all concerned performed admirably. Although the Allies conducted frequent air drops, unaccountably and in spite of promises to the contrary, supplies never contained HMGs or mortars, as these were apparently considered superfluous to the requirements of guerilla warfare. On the eve of the German onslaught only about half of the 4000 maquisards in Vercors were properly armed; there were very few LMGs and bazookas, and rather more shotguns and pistols than rifles or Stenguns.

In an ideal scenario Vercors was vaguely seen by London HQ as a possible strategic bridgehead to be exploited in conjunction with the Normandy landings. *Plan Montagnards*, as the proposed operation was styled, remained tucked away in some drawer. Nonetheless, ambiguous messages from London such as "the alpine chamois heads for the heights" led local maquisards to imagine that the Allies in London and Algiers would firmly support them; that De Gaulle himself would inspect them within days of the Normandy operation, and that a second series of landings would come only a fortnight after D-Day in Normandy. So an ill-inspired Fortress Vercors strategy was implemented.

To make matters worse, Allied HQ in London and Algiers, between whom little love was lost, dithered to a degree. This, it seems, was programmed ambiguity, all part of a deception plan to keep the Germans guessing. Thus when De Gaulle called on the sons of France to rise against the enemy with whatever means at their disposal on 6 June 1944, simultaneous with a general mobilisation decreed by local resistance leaders, the French in Vercors were convinced the time had come to strike a blow against *les Boches*. 24 hours later, however, the mobilisation order was countermanded.

In control of Grenoble since September 1943, the German military authorities had become fully aware of the threat posed by this semi-liberated area and its bands of 'armed terrorists'. Some of the latter, deluding themselves that the Hun was on the run, defiantly hoisted a full-size French tricolor at St-Nizier, as if inviting the enemy to do his worst.

He did. On 12 June a first attack on St-Nizier was repelled, but the Germans returned on the 15th and the maquisards were soon overwhelmed. They withdrew towards Villard-de-Lans, while St-Nizier was torched by its captors. There then ensued a 5-week lull in hostilities.

During this episode forces on the Vercors plateau made ready for the inevitable showdown. On the night of 28-29 June, thirty US Commandos parachuted into Vassieux, ostensibly to organise and train local maquisards, but also to deliver a disquieting message to the effect that Vercors had a low priority rating, and that guerilla forces should aim at disrupting enemy communications and avoid fire-fights. This did not tally with promises of delivery of heavy equipment emanating periodically from Allied HQ, though parachute drops still contained maddeningly few useful weapons. Work was now started on an airstrip at Vassieux where, hopefully, Allied planes would shortly land.

Local Free French leaders also went through the motions of administering a 'liberated' portion of national territory. So a Vercors Republic was proclaimed on 3 July, while full-scale Bastille Day celebrations went ahead, complete with parade and march-past, down at Die, which had also 'liberated' itself. This coincided with a dramatic daylight drop of miscellaneous equipment on Vassieux by a huge formation of Flying Fortresses. The temporary euphoria was seen as extreme provocation by the Germans. Accordingly they bombed and machine-gunned Vassieux and La Chapelle that evening. The massive show of air strength led them to believe that Vercors was going to be reinforced by the Allies.

General Pflaum, the German commander in Grenoble, lost no time marshalling his forces. Numbering some 15,000 men, these included 5 battalions of infantry sealing off the Vercors area, four battalions of mountain troops, an artillery regiment, Feldgendarmerie and SS units, together with the much-feared 'Mongol' auxiliaries – reprisal troops that were sent in to pillage and rape once the SS had done their work. He could also call on unlimited air support, from spotter planes to FW 190 fighter-bombers operating with full impunity from Chabeuil, NW of Vercors. That repeated calls to London to 'take-out' this particular airfield should have gone unheeded, despite unchallenged Allied air superiority, remains one of the mysteries of the Vercors episode. (According to one report, it was bombed 10 days later – too late to materially change the situation).

The long expected German offensive came on 21 July. On a cloudy rainy morning suddenly aircraft appeared over Vassieux. Hopes that they might be Allied were soon dispelled when they were seen to be German. The initial wave, consisting of some 200 glider borne Waffen SS, landed on or near the airstrip and seized the village. Subsequent Free French efforts to dislodge them proved fruitless as further enemy reinforcements arrived. In the course of the fighting Vassieux itself was practically wiped out.

The following day the German attack resumed in earnest. The thrust came S across the Vercors plateau from St-Nizier; another large column headed up the Drôme valley from Crest, but met with stout resistance near Saillans. To the E, the Grimone col was secured, while mountain troops occupied the precipitous E part of Vercors, only thinly held by the resistance, in particular the Pas de la Ville and Pas de l'Aiguille. Near the latter, one can see a plaque commemorating the heroic defence of a cave from which, after vain efforts to blast them out with explosives, a handful of French survivors broke out at night and escaped into Trièves. From the start the fighting had shown that the Germans meant business. On both sides quarter was neither given nor expected. Apart from a few recorded cases where Germans refrained from despatching wounded maquisards, the fare meted out to captured Frenchmen was summary execution.

By Sunday, 23 July the game was up for the Free French. For some unexplained reason the Drôme maquisards had withdrawn from Saillans and Die, where the Mongols were soon to have a field day butchering hospital patients in their beds. All the cols on the E rim of Vercors were firmly held by German alpine troops, and the SS were entrenched in Vassieux. Outflanked on all sides, and with their centre caving in, there was little the Vercors maquisards could do but 'go down first class'.

They did just that. Their feeble defensive line strung out across the plateau, centred on Valchevrière, resisted against fearful odds but finally succumbed to superior firepower. During the closing stages there was fierce hand-to-hand fighting in the course of which the local French commander fended off his attackers with hand grenades to the bitter end rather than surrender. By then the last in a series of forlorn attempts to break through one of the E rim cols had also ended in disaster. That evening Huet sent out a dispersal order to all units and, defeated but undaunted, surviving resistance fighters struggled under cover of darkness to reach the fastnesses of Lente forest, where they went to earth until the hue and cry died down. In a last defiant gesture, before going off the air, Chavant sent a final tragic message to HQ in Algiers, accusing the "criminals and cowards" there of having stood by idly as the Vercors defences crumbled beneath the German onslaught.

At the other end, after this last message had been delayed 3 days in London, and now that it was all over, came a flurry of meetings which revealed that nobody really knew what was happening in Vercors; nor had any reinforcements ever been earmarked for the area. Typically, on the night the plateau was overrun, a small force of paratroopers waited for hours on the tarmac at Algiers, expecting to drop on Vercors, only to have their mission cancelled. Some observers have since suggested that much of the vacillation was due to political in-fighting between Gaullists and Communists, the latter little relishing the thought of a separate portion of France being liberated by De Gaulle's followers.

With their HQ staff in Algiers locked in argument, the Free French on the plateau together with the local Vercors population were being mopped up with a vengeance. For a whole week, massacres, burnings, and other atrocities were the order of the day. In a makeshift field hospital in the Luire caves wounded resistance fighters were despatched by machine gun; some youngsters in La Chapelle were rounded up and shot out of hand, while anybody caught attempting to escape over the Vercors passes was fair game for the Alpine troops or Mongols.

The Fortress Vercors philosophy had apparently failed dismally. Both a strategic and tactical error, it had been a classic case of guerillas getting into the wrong ball-game and attempting large scale operations with inadequate equipment against a better and trained enemy. The outcome was a foregone conclusion. The Germans had enjoyed a brief taste of victory pending their ultimate defeat, in circumstances similar to the forthcoming battle of Arnhem - another instance of the Allies attempting too much, too far, and with too little in the way of firepower and logistic backup.

For the Germans it was a Pyrrhic victory. Not only had they suffered losses, but their will to resist further Allied advances was seriously eroded. After the August landings in Provence, German forces pulled out of most of SE France much earlier than anticipated, largely because they feared attacks on extended lines of communication from other Vercors-style groups of partisans. So, American advance guards rolled into Grenoble within hours of the German evacuation on 21 August, whereas they had only expected to reach it by end September. The price paid by Vercors defenders, though high, would appear to have borne dividends. Emerging from hideouts in Lente forest, many of the survivors managed to be in at the finish when the Allies occupied Grenoble.

After the war, while officialdom conveniently swept its controversial aspects under the carpet, Vercors became a household name, and the story of its exemplary sacrifice became part and parcel of national mythology. "Its martyrdom makes of Vercors an intensely moving symbol...a myth that deserves respect!", announced De Gaulle, to which Marshall De Lattre de Tassigny added: "(Vercors) was a pure and glorious symbol of the French people's struggle for freedom on the home front! "

Contributing to wipe away the shame of the 1940 Armistice and the humiliation of the subsequent occupation, here was a genuine if tragic French military epic – a worthy addition to school text books. The myth transformed Vercors, a practically unknown backwater before 1940, into one of France's most popular centres for outdoor holidays.

Napoleon monument at Laffrey great lake, Matheysine plateau.

VERCORS

Grenoble 210m Occupies one of the finest junction of valleys among mountains in Europe. Thanks in part to the writer Stendhal, who lived here, the first Syndicat d'Initiative (tourist office) in France was opened in Grenoble in 1889. Nowadays a sizeable city, site of several high-tech industries, a kind of alpine Silicon Glen, but rating the second worst pollution levels in the country. All categories of hotels, restaurants, some cheap B & B. Shops and services of all descriptions. No campsite in or near the city centre; the closest is outside the Seyssins suburb, 5km away. Railway station (76.47.50.50/76.87.40.60) is a main terminus with onward connection by the scenically attractive Veynes/Gap line. Coach/bus station nearby (76.47.77.77/76.87.90.31). Information centres at Hôtel du Tourisme, 14 rue de la République (76.42.08.31) or 7 rue Voltaire (76.51.76.00).

GENERAL

Ver = great/high; cor = hill/height. Old Celto-Ligurian tribal name, Vertacomicorii. Looking SW from Grenoble the austere grey cliffs of the Vercors escarpment (often insinuated as the French Dolomites) extend an eastern barrier to the S for 35km, from Moucherotte to Mont Aiguille. It continues round the S perimeter with equally spectacular if less continuous ramparts overlooking the Diois and Royans districts.

A lofty cretaceous limestone pavement, about 400m thick at its core, Vercors has the outwardly daunting aspect of an impregnable citadel - which it is not, as amply demonstrated by history. Moreover it is full of holes, like Gruyère cheese, an unseen subterranean world of bottomless chasms, caves, galleries, lakes and Stygian rivers; a potholer's paradise featuring the third deepest explored cavity in the world - Gouffre Berger (-1142m).

Once the threshold is crossed, either via the Bourne or Furon gorges, we advance through broad vistas of rolling woodland, vast plateaus pockmarked with hamlets and lone farms, and the Montagne de Lans shutting off the eastern horizon. The northern corner of Vercors, part of Isère, comprising Villard-de-Lans, Autrans, Méaudre and Lans, with its temperate climate, is well known and quite densely populated. The southern part, centred on La Chapelle and Vassieux, is an immense empty country with

27

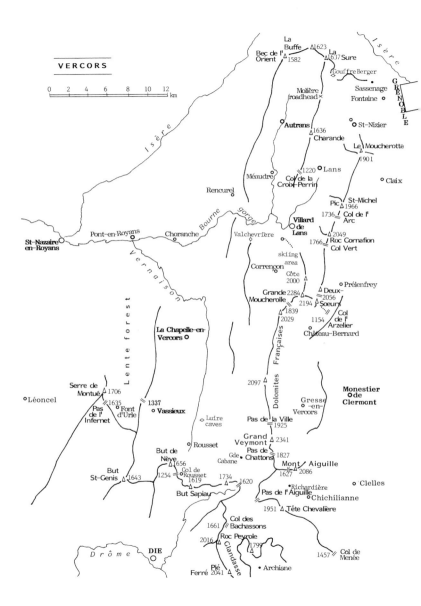

high plateaus of creviced limestone (lapiaz) and extensive forests. Beyond, the blue skies and dry air of Drôme herald an early Mediterranean climate. The cool unpolluted air of the Vercors plateau in summer is acknowledged by the medical profession as outstandingly healthy.

On the W side of the region populated plains merge harmoniously with wooded slopes that soon give way to cliffs and impressive canyons. These spectacular gorges, scoured by the erosion and drainage of centuries, were formerly formidable obstacles to communication. Indeed, the Vernaison (Grands Goulets) and Bourne inlets called for rock climbing to reach the plateau until the early 19th century; the Bourne impasse was then the frontier between Franco-Provençal as spoken in N Vercors, and the patois Provençal of Trièves and Diois to the S. The main gorges are now traversed by roads hacked along and driven through tunnels in rockfaces.

Traditionally an upland region of small farms in the N and trans-humant shepherds in the S, Vercors is one of the few mountain areas in France where symbiosis has been achieved between the conflicting requirements of agriculture, environmentalism and tourism. The rural exodus that has struck many other parts of France seems to have spared Vercors. Farmers are under the aegis of APAP (Association de Promotion des Agriculteurs du Parc), organising collective schemes for stocking grain and dairy products, not to mention a roster system whereby farmers can enjoy holidays on the Riviera! Simultaneously, through diversification, they can derive extra benefit from visitors; many farms provide B & B facilities and offer 'natural' products such as goat cheese. Addressing environmentalist preoccupations, the use of nitrate fertilizers is outlawed. This proved necessary to stave off potential criticism from the shaggy-bearded urban Green brotherhood, who are quite numerous in the Grenoble area.

Since 1970 the Parc Naturel du Vercors has confounded the critics, not only by surviving, but by protecting existing animal species and reintroducing some extinct ones. The last pair of wolves were killed near Villard-de-Lans in 1883, even though one was shot in 1992. A surviving bear seems to have been shot in 1898 at Grande Cabane, at the foot of Grand Veymont, though periodic unconfirmed 'last' sightings were reported in 1914, 1937 and even 1950. In the immediate future it is unlikely that either of these creatures will haunt Vercors forests, and the same must apply for the lynx. For non-carnivores the outlook is much brighter. Corsican mouflon, now numbering about 250, together with a few ibex introduced in 1989, have joined the marmot, chamois, red deer (100 or so) and roe deer. They might be seen fleetingly in Lente forest, or along the E escarpment. Less exciting animals also occur: fox, squirrel, pine-marten, stoat, hare; and some relatively rare birds such as the wall-creeper, Tengmalm's owl, woodcock, ptarmigan, black grouse, short-toed eagle, alongside the endemic assortment of falcons and harriers. For naturalists, walkers and others the PNV has opened some 25 prepared picnic sites (marked on TOP25 and a few other maps), has waymarked scores of forest footpaths, as well as maintaining the long cross country backpacking routes of GR9, 91, 93 and their variants.

Skiing During the 1968 Olympics, the Nordic skiing events were staged at Autrans and Ski-jumping at St-Nizier. Afterwards the Vercors became fashionable as a winter sports venue. Piste skiing had commenced in the area in the early 1930s, when the first skitows appeared at Villard-de-Lans (chiefly frequented by Grenoblois), also at Col de Rousset, catering for skiers from Die. In 1951 Villard inaugurated the Côte-2000 cableway. Another was opened from St-Nizier to the Moucherotte summit in 1955 in conjunction with the then sensational mountain-top Hotel Hermitage. This functioned until 1977 when it went bankrupt. Having been pronounced unsafe, the line was dismantled, but the wreckage is still piled up in the bottom station. The hotel became derelict and closed, though the shell in silhouette presides over the Grenoble scene today.

At present the joint Villard-de-Lans/Corrençon skiing area, astride the NW slopes of Grande Moucherolle, is by far the most extensive in the Vercors massif. A bit too organised, perhaps, with 100 ski instructors, large carparks and bossy attendants, it apes the big impersonal and unfriendly resorts of Isère and Savoy without quite succeeding in producing their panache. The lack of snow in recent years has been crippling; the terrain has required incessant bombardment by over 100 snow-cannon to guarantee bump-free (sometimes stony) smooth skiing around the top station of the cableway, though there are steeper, more pleasant runs down through the forest and back to the resort.

Also dependent on snow-cannon, Gresse-en-Vercors village resort has been similarly affected by dry winters. Enjoying marginally better snow cover and closer to Grenoble, Lans-en-Vercors is ideal for a day's skiing. Col de Rousset, now the biggest resort in Drôme, has skilifts culminating at the But Sapiau. Finally, Font d'Urle has a few skitows and 20km of prepared slopes. These last 2 centres are too far S to see much snow, and are heavily in debt; the same applies to Gresse, which has invested lavishly in the 'Dolomites Françaises' residential complex and is years away from getting in the black.

Col de l'Arzelier, Col de Menée, St-Nizier and Méaudre also offer limited downhill skiing, but the last named is better known as a Nordic skiing centre. This activity is the most popular winter sport in Vercors, and nearby Autrans is the langlauf Mecca. Two world famous events are held here every winter: the 424km Foulée Blanche, and the slightly longer Grande Trace (534km). Other venues for cross-country include Villard-de-Lans and Corrençon, with their historically famous Valchevrière course; Rencurel, St-Martin, La Chapelle, Vassieux and the vastness of the Lente forest. But cross-country is not quite the bread winner the locals would like it to be, and most resorts have introduced a pass system which doesn't really fleece the skier, yet allegedly finances piste maintenance.

Villard-de-Lans 1020m Pop.4100. Grenoble 32km, Valence 70km, Die 65km, Lyon 130km. All main services, about 28 hotels in all categories, B & B houses, numerous restaurants, etc. Huge parking area close to town centre, combined with bus station. Gîte/bunkhouse 2km S of centre, on a side road to E of junction called the Balmette. Municipal campsite at Font Noire, off N access road (76.95.14.77). Caters equally for summer and winter visitors with organised trips and courses in every type of outdoor/sporting activity; tourist office (76.95.10.38). To the S, an 18-hole golf course with clubhouse is laid out at Corrençon. Cableway (Côte-2000) with summer/winter operation from Balcon de Villard (1150m), 4km S of town (bus/taxi), to 1720m; operates with a lunchtime break from 9.00am to 6.30pm; guidebook parties have arrived sooner to find the engineer will start immediately; see especially hereafter, Grande Moucherolle.

GOUFFRE BERGER   1460m

At one time the deepest known cavity in the world (-1442m). It forms part of a complex underground hydro-geological network that links up with Les Cuves de Sassenage - a series of cave openings W of Grenoble - long famous as the legendary home of Mélusine the fairy, and one of the classic wonders of Dauphiné.

From 1953 to 1956 the gouffre was explored by potholers from the CAF-Grenoble, who had long suspected that the Sornin plateau run-off somehow reached the Sassenage caves. A first world record of -1122m was set up at the time. Between 1966 and 1968 further exploration was undertaken by a British team led by Ken Pearce, followed by members of a Parisian club. Since then it has become a regular fixture, but the cavers you may see there on a Sunday afternoon are probably not the genuine article.

A classic outing for Grenoblois, the cave entrance is easily attainable from the Molière roadhead. By car, via N531 to Lans-en-Vercors, then up D106 to Col de la Croix-Perrin, café (1218m). Turn off along narrow winding horizontal forestry road, potholed and tricky in parts with lots of blind bends, to reach eventually a large clearing with a surfaced road R(NE) at 1522m. Follow this to Molière parking area (1632m); orientation table and notable viewpoint. Access is easier from Autrans by D218 to join the other end of the forestry road just before D218 goes into the (now closed) Mortier tunnel; return S along forestry road to the fork at 1522m. Often busy on a Sunday with picnickers ambling off over the Sornin plateau, or into neighbouring forest, usually with dogs and children in attendance. Superlative views over the Alps from Mont Blanc to Belledonne, Taillefer, Oisans and Dévoluy, make it worthwhile.

This marvellous location explains why Grenoble-based sports outfitters use the homely Molière pasture setting combined with the tremendous mountainscape backcloth for phoney 'wilderness' illustration purporting to show their tents and other equipment in a vibrant extreme situation.

For those entirely on foot, go to Engins hamlet below Lans-en-Vercors by bus and follow the plainly marked GR9 track to pt. 1495 (see below), 2h.

From carpark head N (gate) across grassy plateau along well marked track. After 800m a wire fence is negotiated; now turn R(E) by a path that descends towards the forest, passes a typical Vercors glacière containing snow till early summer (and graffiti allegedly left there by Napoleonic troops) then veers NE through mainly coniferous forest. As the way is now tricky to find, route finding skills become essential; if unfamiliar with the ground, do not try it in poor visibility. Faint red waymarks, few and far between, lead on across clearings of grass and lapiaz; in 1993, red and white plastic markers had been tied to branches.

Continue the gradual descent NE in woods to a sharp bend in a clearing where other paths arrive from the W and NW. Resume descent through woods with limestone pavement to junction with GR9 at 1530m. (Possible, on way back, to take GR9 from here to Sornin hut, then follow variant down through woods to Fournel hamlet, a convenient place to be picked up by a recovery vehicle). Now go L(N) down the GR for about 130m to a sharp bend L in a clearing. At this spot a small path forks R(N), pt.1495, along the top of a rockband. Follow it for 400m, rising a little, then cut off L at a cairn and red blobs (where path still continues ahead). Terrain is most misleading; you will doubtless meet other hikers milling round aimlessly. Wind down over slabby rocks, curving R to tree-fringed limestone hollow where cave entrance is at last found. No guardrail, but wooden poles lie across the chasm to which cavers fix pulleys when needed. Memorial plaques to victims claimed by Gouffre Berger (1h from carpark, allow 1h30 for gradually ascending return; 2h30 from Engins for those who who came by bus, 1h45 to go back).

Variation: On rejoining GR9 follow its waymarks W over pavé to clearing pt.1547, where it turns sharp R (NNW). Instead, take a path straightahead in a cutting through the woods rising to the Plénouze meadow where the main bridleway S leads back to Molière roadhead.

CHARANDE 1709m

Though the highest point on the escarpment round Autrans, probably the least interesting. Popular with walkers, horse riders and mountain bikers.

From Molière roadhead carpark (see Gouffre Berger, above), ascend wooded ridge S, across a saddle, and go on without incident to a narrow grass strip alongside the forest; a wooden pole marks summit (30 min). Carry on along the pleasant edge, down to the Ours col (1649m), with a rocky gully on its E side. Ahead, ascend the wooded ridge over pt.1686 (fallen trees) and and come down to Pas de Bellecombe (1636m), signpost, etc (30 min). Descend path NE, through a gate, to the Robertière pasture below and follow riders' trail in grass NNE over a brow and down to a private chalet. The path becomes a 4WD track in the pasture; follow it for 1.25km, and after passing below Charande go ahead where it makes a circuit L. Rejoin the track but soon leave it for a little path on the L, rising directly to the Molière source (drinking troughs for cows) and carpark (1h, round trip 2h).

LA BUFFE 1623m

Promontory and gentle pyramid marking the extreme NE corner of the Vercors escarpment and a special viewpoint commanding a vast panorama over the Chartreuse, Belledonne and other Dauphiné peaks.

From Autrans (1042m) the D218 road leads N in 8.5km to the Mortier tunnel (closed); 100m before the entrance, a tarmac forestry road (1389m) circles round NW/SE above tunnel entrance; 250m along this road, parking on grass and stones on outer edge; 50m further up, small signpost indicating where path starts. Follow clear path N in forest, ignoring a fork R, and going straight up steeply to the cliff edge at a flat spot on GR9, waymarks. Go R(E) for a few min to cleared summit site (45 min from road).

Another slightly longer way is possible from Refuge de Gève roadhead (1286m), attainable from Autrans. Follow GTA path N through forest to Pas de la Clé (1509m), whence top of the Buffe is reached by keeping close to ridge along GR9 that overlooks La Grande Brèche scree-slide (2h).

LA SURE 1643m

1.5km SE of La Buffe, the next pronounced summit on the wooded escarpment edge, easily combined with former to make a little circuit. From La Buffe follow GR9 path along the edge and in undergrowth down to the Pas du Mortier (1543m). Continue at a moderate gradient SE to T junction in a clearing; go L up to the crest line and follow this to wooden summit post, 45 min from La Buffe. For descent to tunnel entrance, return to T junction and descend a woodland path SW to the forestry road at c1460m. [This path carries on down below road to the Poya forestry hut (1294m) on the D218, about one km below tunnel]. Now go N along road to where La Buffe path starts.

Plénouze 1648m An elevated pasture 3 km S of La Sure, on the stretch of ridge S of GR9 and traversed by a path called the Sentier des Génisses (Heifers' path). Rock outcrops on SW side offer short practice rock climbs, frequented by parties from Autrans.

BEC DE L'ORIENT 1554/1568m

Headland marking the extreme NW corner of Vercors escarpment. Celebrated viewpoint, though less revealing than La Buffe. N of Autrans, 2 forestry roads enter a huge wooded area; the Nave one, parallel with and below GR9, can be followed delicately with a small car for 5km to its end in a small clearing at 1435m. The other, a metalled road further E, leads easily for 5km to the Gève hut (1286m), at N end of the large Pré de Gève meadow.

From the first roadhead continue by a good path due N across the Nave meadows to a little saddle (1527m) above the escarpment cliffs where, in 20m, GR9 is joined. Follow the good waymarked trail R, coming round N again to the cliff edge where it is cut by a big chimney/gully. Carry on near edge to a large iron cross (1554m) marking the first summit. Path then turns R(E) along the edge to skirt pt. 1568 in the wood (1h from roadhead).

From the Gève hut proceed N along forest track to the Cyclone clearing where the track ends (1352m). Go off L(NW) in the wood, ignoring the first L fork, till a clearing is reached in 10 min. Where the path turns N, go off L(NW) over the top part of the clearing into the wood again. After 5 min take a vague fork R(N) and in 250m distance go up gently to the cliff edge at the Pas Brochier (1452m) (1h). Now follow GR9 path W, closely along the edge and exposed in places, to the summit in another 15 min.

Autrans   1042m   Tourist office (76.95.30.70). All main services and campsites. Since 1909, Autrans and the surrounding plateau has been home to hundreds and, more recently, thousands of cross-country skiers. After the boost afforded by the 1968 Winter Olympics, Autrans has regularly hosted prestige events such as the Foulée Blanche and the French Nordic Skiing Championships. Native talent has achieved universal acknowledgement with at least one Olympic coach and several top-flight contenders hailing from Autrans. Nor is downhill skiing neglected; there are numerous skilifts and slopes that, apart from being 'prepared' for use by winter skiers, have been carefully planted with grass like lawns so that summer vacationers don't have to put up with conspicuous eye-sores in the landscape and can actually enjoy leisurely strolls on a pleasant surface.

This respect for the environment is reflected elsewhere. Resort authorities have gone to great pains to preserve the friendly village atmosphere so many visitors search for. While numerous modern *résidences* have been built, an attempt has been made to respect distinctive Vercors style architecture, and there are very few of those jerry-built monstrosities one sees in ski centres all over the Alps. Some 8000 beds are available in guest house, gîte, or residence accommodation; emphasis is laid upon creating a neighbourly approach calculated to establish a Vercors brand image. Recommended is the hotel-restaurant Au Feu de Bois; good local cuisine and dishes at reasonable prices (76.95.33.32). All told, a quiet and engaging little resort to which people want to return.

– o –

LE MOUCHEROTTE   1901m

With its magnificent sweep of apparently vertical cliff towering high above Grenoble, this is one of the city's most distinctive landmarks and a classic outing for locals. Easily attained on foot from St-Nizier village (reached by the broad, winding D106 in

30-40 min depending on conditions; bus service).

From St-Nizier-du-Moucherotte. On foot or ski (before end March), recommended. From centre of St-Nizier (1150m) the D106f describes a rough rectangle round a sloping field fleetingly used for skiing (Jan-Feb; couple of skitows). Huge parking area beside abandoned cableway station. Strike SE along a lane and and turn R onto GR91 near some houses. Now up lane SSW and pass huge (unseen) ski-jump bowl of 1968 Olympics, after which the track of GR91 enters forest and goes into a broad, comparatively treeless NW-facing gully. Fairly steep slopes require considerable exertion, levelling out at c1400m where the GR becomes a broad, comfortable track. It heads W and emerges at a sharp R-hand turn. Les Trois Pucelles (1456m), a popular rock climbing site, are seen nearby to the NE, while terminal cliffs of Moucherotte loom to the S. The track rises in coniferous forest for a short way across the E flank of the mountain; later, after a couple of steep turns, it switches to the W flank for a gradually ascending traverse of more than one km (tough going for the unfit spring skier, but easy on foot in summer) to a point where the GR swings sharply L to ascend the final forest slopes in a NW direction. Cross a wooded saddle, leaving derelict hotel on L for a last rocky patch before ridge and summit are attained. Orientation table (2h30-3h from St-Nizier).

Shorter summer (and easy winter) route. Above Lans-en-Vercors, a good side road D106i mounts to La Sierre 'Stade de Neige' (1400m), large parking area and restaurant. From N end of this facility, GR91 goes off NNE at a moderate gradient in forest and eventually across open slopes to summit in 5km (2h).

Descent on ski. Cross saddle in general NNE direction, in line of old cableway, and ski down a magnificent clearing that comes out on GR91 track. Now reverse ascent route, making short excursions on slopes L(W) of track, first heading N, then W, till large NW-facing gully is reached. This yields the most satisfactory run of the day, right down past the skitow to the gîte d'étape at La Tour on the D106 road; walk back N some 600m to St-Nizier.

From Le Haut Seyssins by E flank and Château Bouvier. A more arduous undertaking because it starts from much lower down (594m), while the upper portion necessitates a good head for heights and adequate footwear though no real difficulties are encountered.

Turn off L from D106 (Grenoble to St-Nizier) road and go up into Haut Seyssins (bus stop); park car as high as possible. Woodland footpath strikes S, then steeply SW (after ignoring L-hand variant linking up with Bouveyres), to join another path coming in from N at pt.1112; so reach the Vercors perimeter path (Balcon Est,blue/yellow/blue flashes). This is followed NW for one km to a fork at c1250m immediately below Moucherotte. Turn sharp L and wind up S, later crossing a ravine of the Bessay stream. Higher up, leave the technically more arduous Vallon des Forges itinerary heading NW, and go straight on via the Chemin des Bouvières (Cow-girls path); signpost, yellow waymarks. Path now works round the Château Bouvier rock (1543m) above, and goes up onto E spur of the Moucherotte; ignore another variant (R-hand turning for Vallier grotto). Take a series of sharp zags, cable in one place, then a gradual plod on excellent path up steep stony slopes interspersed with stunted pine, to emerge very close to abandoned summit hotel (4h-4h30 from Haut Seyssins).

Variation. A much shorter way of going up this E side of the mountain, and recommended for making a traverse combined with the St-Nizier route, is to start from the prominent bend at pt.1092 on the D106; this woodland spot (bus stop) is known as the Pucelles picnic site, along a lane running S then W/NW. A few paces into lane, waymarked start on L of the Balcon Est perimeter path. Follow this pleasantly S in forest with a moderate ascent for 2.5km to the fork at c1250m where the route from Haut Seyssins is joined and the Balcon Est trail is quitted. Saves some 1h-1h15 in total time.

PIC SAINT MICHEL 1966m

Attractive promontory on the Vercors E rim some distance S of Moucherotte, much frequented by ski tourers and summer ramblers alike. Recommended. Suitable walking routes from E and W sides both by way of Col de l'Arc (1736m).

E slope. No access by public transport. Drive S from Grenoble, turning off R from Sisteron motorway at Claix village. Follow on up past Jayères along a winding road and turn L at junction (736m), through forest and fields past St-Ange hamlet, before a further turn L. Go on till metalled road runs out; keep going a bit further till Pré du Four carpark is reached on gravel and grass (1230m).

Path heads off W across Pré du Four (meadow of the oven); the antiquated oven itself may be visited, just L of path; this is as fine a stretch of grass as one might expect to find in Vercors. On entering forest climb sharply to join E perimeter path (Balcon

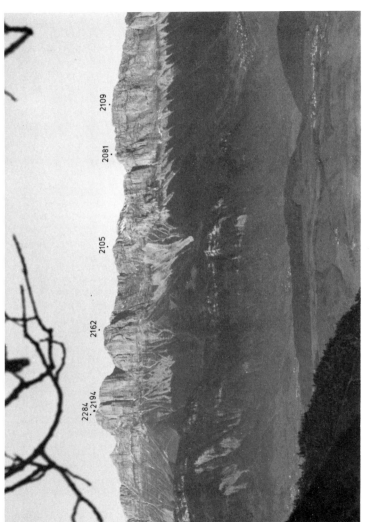

Les Deux-Soeurs and Gerbier section of Vercors E escarpment.

Est) at 1360m, some 700m distance from carpark. Carry on to a sharp bend R (near pt.1426) leading to a gently ascending traverse WSW through forest. Emerge above the treeline below the moderately steep terminal slopes of grass and stones leading from pt.1571 to Col de l'Arc (1736m), which is attained after a series of zigzags (2h15 from carpark). A busy spot on Sundays in fair weather. Apart from parties seen on same route, others are departing, arriving or visibly picnicking on all sides.

Summit is now approached by following easy, well marked path that mounts NNE along pleasant ridge (45 min from col, about 3h from carpark).

In September huntsmen may have been out in force after grouse, chamois and imported Corsican mouflon. Many of their dogs, only too eager to join the fray and carried away by enthusiasm, contrive to get lost in the woods. On the way back to carpark be prepared to see one or more of these ferocious looking hunters waiting dejectedly in the forest for their canine companions to turn up!

W slope. Generally more popular with day-trippers, slightly shorter, and the start can be almost reached by bus. On the D106 outside Lans-en-Vercors a good surfaced road forks SE at Les Bernards (1041m) towards La Sierre 'Stade de Neige'. (500m along this on the L is a big cliff, Bec de Cornillon, with nice rock climbs). Go up it for 3km to large parking area just before final hairpin (1280m) below the 'Stade'; signpost at this bend. From here follow GR91 footpath due S through forest to a meadow at Les Allières and the Collet du Furon (1449m). Go on briefly through a couple of clearings and keep L(SE), away from a grassy track. Work through a stretch of forest along a cobbly path to the Font Froide spring from where it mounts moderately steep slopes in scrub and scree. Near the top avoid a rockband and circle round in a broad hollow to the Col de l'Arc (2h, or 2h45 on foot from main road). Continue up ridge to top in 45 min.

W slope on ski. Normally done along a piste track in forest due S of La Sierre (pt.1472, 1615). This track becomes a tiny path (in summer), at a moderate gradient and leading in a long shallow trough called Combe Oursière to steeper open slopes directly under W side of summit. Ascend these slopes, avoiding little outcrops and rockbands, to top; popular ascent for March/April.

Top: Roc Cornafion and Col Vert on R, from Côte-2000 cableway top station.
Bottom: Gerbier pinnacle/pillars called Les Sultanes, adjoining Pas de l'Oeille on R. Seen from above Côte-2000 cableway top station.

ROC CORNAFION 2049m

Shapely, conspicuous rock pyramid when seen from Villard-de-Lans, one of the more distinctive tops of the Vercors E rim, and possibly of greater interest to the climber. Stiff scramble at the finish with 20m of I+/II- rock work to summit.

On E outskirts of Villard-de-Lans, carpark near Les Cochettes skitow (1084m); 30 min on foot. Head S to join GR91 footpath that climbs SE through forest, linking up after 1.5km at pt.1361 with another path, also from Les Cochettes. The going gets a bit steeper, then emerges in a broad clearing (wire fence) where the Refuge de Roybon lies (1450m); Cornafion's majestic pyramid seen to good advantage from here (1h30). Continue E up through forest and eventually grassy slopes with a few zags to Col Vert (1766m) (1h).

A path traverses steep slopes on the Grenoble (E) side. Follow this N, narrow and rocky in places for over one km, reascending to below summit line. Waymarked junction at continuation of perimeter path NNE to Col de l'Arc. Fork L(W) for the last stiff scramble to reach first top. Summit proper is a few m further S along ridge; exposed scramble, grade II-; uninitiated should be roped (1h30 from Col Vert, 4h from Les Cochettes, 4h30 from Villard centre).

Another access is possible from La Conversarie roadhead out of Villard, further N, with a well marked path via Col de l'Arc to the E perimeter (Balcon) path. An approach from the Grenoble (E) side via Prélenfrey to the Balcon path takes about the same time.

Roc Cornafion W slopes on ski, Combe Chaulange run. An ideal short outing on ski, January/March. From Villard-de-Lans go NE past Les Lombards and Les Nobles to park car just short of Les Eymards; taxi will go here. Strike SSE across woods and fields (Prairies de Machiret). After crossing La Conversarie to Col de l'Arc path, tedious going in forest due to undergrowth. Then tackle steeper slopes to work round end of a rockband into the lower part of Combe Chaulange. Shortly after emerging from forest, GR91 is passed, and progress up gentler slopes, studded with occasional pines, with Cornafion's magnificently snow plastered rock buttresses above. Sticking to R-hand side of Combe and heading SE, eventually trend R(S) and zigzag up steepening slopes to a large shoulder (1855-1906m) immediately below summit pyramid, on W side. Steep slopes lie to the S, offering possibility of a fine run to Roybon hut (feasible if a party has arranged to be picked up near Les Cochettes).

Grande Moucherolle normal route from last saddle under summit pile.

Otherwise, return by Combe Chaulange which affords relatively trouble-free skiing till after GR91 has been passed, whence the descent requires precise skiing on the path that slants away W towards La Conversarie roadhead, till wire fence at bottom end of forest is reached. It is now advisable to traverse fields and woods NNE back towards Les Eymards – a bit rough on skis, so maybe walk (about 5h for round trip).

GRANDE MOUCHEROLLE 2284m

Second highest elevation in Vercors. Due to its strategic position at a prominent kink in the E rim, and unlike some of its neighbours which are mere ridges, has something of the looks and atmosphere of a major peak. At once a sharp fang when seen from the Matheysine tops (E), and a handsome summit with cupola-like profile when observed from the Lans plateau. Unsurprisingly the focus of several routes. Its satellites, the Deux Soeurs and other precipitous neighbours of the Gerbier cliffs are famous rock climbing venues, all adding interest to the group.

North side normal route. Fine terminal ridge with 6m of grade I+. Otherwise walking, highly recommended. The approach is rendered tedious by the extent of ski piste development for the Côte-2000 resort, but which has to be accepted as a necessary evil by peak-baggers. From Villard-de-Lans go to Balcon de Villard, 1150m (Côte-2000), bus service. Vast carpark area and restaurants. Cableway functions throughout summer and avoids all the lower slopes, carved up with piste tracks; top station at 1720m. From here, just L(E) of a ridge line, follow plain broad track S, soon with a sharp R turn (signpost) and more bends L and R under W side of a low relief ridge; it leads to a platform area, the true Côte-2000. Closed hut, piste signboard, etc (1h).

From hut bear further R(W) and find hidden broad zigzag in the piste track descending round a steep rubble slope and returning L(SE) below it; poles border outer edge of this circular route. Go on S, still losing a little height, and now some way below the Jaux ridge above, till a steep, unmarked little path forks L about 150m distance from a small hut and signboard at c1900m. Ascend this steep path for a couple of min to where it eases off in a long platform overlooking the Ourson junction. Follow it S with a moderate ascent to rejoin stony track coming from junction below. Continue ahead to a turn R, then L again to a stony platform area between 2 skitow pylons. Just above, a small path runs L to R in grass from the Col des Deux Soeurs to a saddle below the summit pile of the mountain. Go along this

View E of High Dauphiné from Grande Moucherolle summit. Far L, Aiguilles d'Arves (65km); L-centre, Râteau/La Meije (60km); R-centre, Barre des Ecrins (65km); far R, L'Olan (53km).

pleasantly due W to fine saddle (c2150m) (1h15). Impressive display of cliffs on L.

Directly above, climb the E facet by a narrow stony path trending L then R to a tiny terrace area on R side. Go up diagonally L using big cut steps in the turf of a hanging grass field, to enter shallow chimney/gully just under the E ridge proper (a direct way comes up this rather loose chimney). Go up chimney with large holds for 20m to where it almost merges with ridge on L. Climb the last 4-6m by bridging (I+) to exit delicately (some loose rock) on a large platform. Continue airily along a sharp, almost horizontal broken crest to summit 75m away (30 min, 2h45 to 3h from cableway top station). Superb view of high peaks in the Écrins massif and of Mont Blanc.

A popular and longer variation from the hut at Côte-2000 site, signposted *par les Crêtes*, follows the Rochers des Jaux crest with a little track to Col des Deux Soeurs and needs an extra hour.

WSW Ridge by Refuge de l'Ours. Similarly approached from the N, longer than the normal route, more sporting and remote, with bits of I+ on ridge proper. Ideal for a traverse. As for normal route, to reach the Ourson hut/signboard, near pt.1916 (1h15). Follow branch track W, winding round a large bare hillock (1994m) to a fork. Keep R and descend W and NW in the Ourson depression and so round toe of NW ridge at c1790m. Round the corner, a path L(SSE) hugs the base of the NW ridge and climbs quickly to a rocky headslope and the Col des Moucherolles (2086m) (1h30). Go up ridge (old blue flashes); it soon steepens in rock; traverse below crest on R(S) side to a gully; go up this and exit L towards crest until a ledge line in rocks mounts R to reach crest at a large cairn (several movements of I+). Continue briefly by the broad ridge to summit (45 min, 3h30-4h from cableway station).

NW Ridge. The base is crossed on previous route. The most sporting way up, only a couple of short grade II pitches, steep in places, sometimes exposed, fine holes right through one ridge step.

Deux Soeurs – Moucherolle traverse. Relatively ambitious outing for good summer conditions, recommended to experienced mountain scramblers. Bits of grade I+. Delicate descent. The route ascends the great couloir between the two monolithic cliffs of Agathe and Sophie, together known as the Deux Soeurs. The approach from the Arzelier col goes right up underneath the famous 300m high Spigolo prow of Agathe, first climbed by Serge Coupé and party in 1960.

from SE

DEUX-SOEURS

Agathe

2194 • 2193 •

Spigolo SE

COL 2056

2162 Sophie •

to 1309 carpark

Cave

Balcon Est Path

gîte

1420

Bruyères chairlift—Arzelier col

With a car. From Grenoble by the N75 to the S outskirts of Vif. Turn R onto D8 past La Ferrière and Les Petits Amieux to Saint Barthélemy. Then wind through forest up to and through Prélenfrey. Forest road ascends into Gua Communal forest, to roadhead at pt.1309 beneath jagged Gerbier ridge and cliffs.

Take broad track up through woods; blue signpost: Col des Deux Soeurs 2h. After 300m or so leave track and take an obvious narrow path signposted: Baraque des Clos. Keep an eye open for falling logs; foresters are active in area (warning notice to this effect). Emerge above treeline, cross some loose scree and bushes to reach the Baraque des Clos, a rather shabby-looking hut half-embedded in a big boulder near a conspicuous clump of larch (45 min). From hut ignore Balcon Est path on R; go up L to next intersection. Leave Pas de l'Oeille path on R and keep L again, crossing head of steep gully on friable limestone (spring) to continue due S along gently rising path over moderate grass slopes with some deciduous growth and stunted pine. At end of riser start a series of zags to foot of Deux Soeurs, whence good view is to be had of Col de l'Arzelier and ski installations below.

Now follow ledge trail L(S), yellow flashes, working along limestone band at base of cliffs. This section is a bit exposed in a couple of places (cable), with occasional overhangs where tall people with bulky sacks must stoop. Pass entrance to a prominent cave on R, then to a fork with continuation S of ledgeline and start of way up great gully above, on R.

By bus, to Col de l'Arzelier (1154m); hotel, restaurant, bar, and Bruyères chairlift to 1470m, just below Arzelier gîte chalet (dormitory/beds) at top of forest. From here follow waymarked path slanting L up large grass slope under the magnificent pillar of Agathe. Cross the Balcon Est path to reach base of pillar by a series of zigzags to c1800m. Work R(N) along narrow terraces, rising from one level to the next with increasing exposure to join the previous approach as it enters the Deux Soeurs couloir (1h45 from top of chairlift, 2h45 from Col de l'Arzelier).

Climb the Deux Soeurs gully by easy limestone steps in zigzags, quite pleasant and always interesting with cables in places, to exit at the Col des Deux Soeurs (2056m), closed by an incongruous metal fence, apparently designed to keep skiers from tumbling over the edge in winter (2h15 from 1309 roadhead; 2h15 from top of chairlift; 3h15 from Col de l'Arzelier).

Now climb the Grande Moucherolle as described in the normal route (45 min). Continue along WSW ridge by gently descending path. One can now make out upper portion of Corrençon ski area with Petite Moucherolle (2156m) slightly to the L, also with a skilift right to the top. A little before end of summit ridge, leave it at a conspicuous cairn and follow blue waymarks and narrow trod that veers sharply L, down a steep rocky section. Traverse initially SE, then follow on down a S-facing gully; a bit steep and narrow in places but no problem by following blue waymarks. So reach Col des Moucherolles (2086m) (30 min). To avoid contact with ski-development, go on over grassy slopes and slippery rock, traverse an unpleasant shale slope, and start up NE side of Petite Moucherolle by a gully full of loose scree. Traverse over top of the Petite and continue to Roche du Coin (1991m) close to top station of Corrençon chairlift, right up by edge of escarpment lined with unsightly ski-fences. Now descend rough slope SW to Pas de la Balme (1839m) (1h30 from Gde. Moucherolle).

Ahead, traverse SW across the rockface under the escarpment edge, waymarked, to a spot directly under pt.1929. Now go down a fairly good trace in the rocks (Mur des Sarrasins) to steep broken rock slopes with grass in which the waymarked line makes zigzags trending L(E), then in a long sweep R(SW), before reaching with further twists the perimeter path at pt.1558 (1h).

Now follow the perimeter path E across steep ground just above the treeline, to grassy spur not far above the Arzelier hut and chairlift (4km, 1h15). Descend by the latter, or to reach forest parking pt.1309 continue along the Balcon Est, N to the Baraque des Clos (3h30 from Pas de la Balme; round trip at least 7h30).

Note: The ridge along top of the Mur des Sarrasins marks the supposed site of a defensive wall still visible today built by Vercors defenders at the time of Saracen invasions about the year 920.

Variation. Return from top of Grande Moucherolle to the Deux Soeurs col. From here ascend the plain rock and grass ridge slope of Sophie, cross its summit (2162m) and traverse the main ridge N, towards the end keeping below crest on L side, to the **Pas de l'Oeille** (1960m); descend from there to the Balcon Est path, while a little path on the W side traverses round to the top station of the Côte-2000 cableway above Villard. On most parts there is steep ground with short sections graded I+.

- o -

Gresse-en-Vercors 1190m Agreeable small village resort on D8a, modest hotel/restaurant, B & B, general store. 1.5km W along good road D8d, La Ville hamlet, more shops, small hotels, B & B, restaurants; campsite; this is local ski centre, fully open in summer. About 200m before roadhead (L branch), Maison du Parc hut with dormitory for 30, self-catering room, wash room/ showers, toilets, similar to an unwardened CAF hut. If door is locked, inquire at M du P office adjoining. This is an economic base for the entire area, including Mont Aiguille, for those with a car. Large parking spaces. Taxi available from Gresse, 2.5km away.

GRAND VEYMONT 2341m

Formerly Grand Vêhemont, an ancient name reputedly of Celtic origin, perhaps used as a natural altar by Druids in Gallic times. Splendid, majestic summit, the highest peak in Vercors, thus regularly visited by walkers in summer. Contrasting features are the syncline slope fringed with cliff-bands on the remote W side, and huge buttressed crags some 400m high facing E and conspicuously visible from N75 road between the Lus col and Clelles. The pale rose limestone is of poor quality and yields few, rarely repeated climbs. Of these, the R-hand buttress was first ascended deviously in 1952. First actual ascent of the mountain cannot be determined because hunters have been frequent visitors for 3 centuries. First modern British ascent by W A B Coolidge, F Gardiner with Simon Barnéoud, 21 September 1888. (Gervais de Tilbury, an Englishman living in Provence, is supposed to have climbed it in 1211; he also first reported the existence of Mont Aiguille). Treated with respect by sane ski tourers because of the hidden fringe of cliff along underside of the large tilted slope that characterises the W side. Extreme skiers sometimes descend a NE couloir just S of Pas de la Ville.

North Ridge. Normal route, a classic Vercors excursion, highly recommended. Simple mountain walking with 40m of grade I-/I scrambling. From the roadhead just beyond Maison du Parc hut (1245m), signpost: Grand Veymont 3h45. Follow stony lane SW for one km into stunted pine woodland where the path mounts steeply past spring on R, then through mixed forest of pine and deciduous trees. After a prominent bend R(N) emerge on pasture; follow zigzags trending L over gentle grassy slopes between hillocks. At c1700m cross the small but obvious Balcon Est path running N-S. Continue ascending towards the pass ahead; soon keep L to work above scree over a stony part degraded by people short-cutting in descent. So make a rising traverse into a little corner (plaque) and move up R again into narrow opening of Pas de la Ville (1925m, 2h30). Park noticeboard, cairns, wooden cross and plaque commemorating victims of WW2. In summer, early risers may be rewarded with ibex sighting in vicinity.

Descending the roof of Grand Veymont N ridge. Grande Moucherolle, far R.

Grand Veymont, E face cliffs.

View E over flattish Vercors plateau, densely forested in this sector. The ridge above is a mix of grassy patches, limestone ribs and intervening scree gullies. In damp conditions the first 100m can become quite slippery; otherwise simple walking.

Climb steep twisting path cut in flank of ridge. After 50m the the path line slants in bare rock, at 2 points touching ridge crest, but generally on the flank; steep and dangerous for the unwary in damp conditions. If you reach this spot before 8.00am, verglas might be found. With a final movement R, finish up a broad open scree gully at the lower end of a grassy trench formed between 2 ribs of the ridge. Go up path pleasantly to huge inclined grassy roof of mountain forming W side of ridge. The clear path mounts this somewhat tediously, eventually crossing the head of deep gully exits on L; after more tedium it reaches the cairned summit (1h30, 4h from roadhead).

In high season the summit resembles Trafalgar Square. Curious tantalising view of the nearby and considerably lower Mt Aiguille, where you are unlikely to see more than a couple of tiny silhouetted figures.

W side approach from St-Agnan. Though latter hamlet can be reached by bus, you need a car or taxi to get to Coche roadhead carpark. From St-Agnan (2 inns, shop, gîte, camping) at D518/D103 junction, drive further S along D518 to unmarked turning L(E) at pt.897. Go up narrow, winding, poorly-surfaced lane through Coche forest to picnic and parking area near the Coche forestry hut (1348m).

[Along the E side of D518, note outstanding rock climbers' pinnacle thrusting up through the forest, called simply the Aiguille Rocher; and an earlier turning for the famous Luire cave used as a hospital by the French in the 1944 uprising; parking and guided tours, quite expensive].

From Coche parking head S past a vehicle barrier to Pré Grandu forestry building. Now turn off E along Combau track, through a few small clearings in forest and climbing steadily to the large Pichet clearing at pt.1477, where the track divides. Bear L (waymarks) and rise NE in a depression, steering E after one km to reach the large open area of Chau with small closed private hut of Nouvelle Jasse de la Chau; Chau spring is nearby (1h45 from carpark). From the 1614m crossroads beyond, follow clear path E with blue/yellow flashes (Sentier Central) through undergrowth and stunted trees to rocky ground and a stonefield where the good path zigzags up steeply to finish at the Pas de la Ville (1h, 2h45 from Coche).

This approach is much frequented in summer; almost as popular as the one from Gresse. The military regularly indulge in war games up here, charging about in battle dress and making a nuisance of themselves.

South Ridge. More sporting and more interesting than the N ridge but considerably longer, depending on approach taken. Has a gully-staircase section of I+. Note, parties should not camp or bivouac at the tempting Grande Cabane site (1563m), normally occupied by shepherds and their animals (dogs forbidden). Pay heed to the weather; the Coche and Rousset roadheads have noticeboards with a warning about the dangers to parties lost (and fatalities) on the bleak Vercors high plateaux; map and a good compass essential.

From the Coche roadhead (1348m, see above) proceed as for the Pas de la Ville and N ridge, as far as crossroads 1614m (1h45). Go SE and S along GR91, into denser forest and over limestone pavement to stone piles marking former site of the Serrons barn (1670m). Leave GR91 here and take a small path branching L (SE) across a scrubby clearing then again in forest, through vague cuttings (area called Bonnevau) to emerge at pt.1727 on path coming from the Grande Cabane to Pas de Chattons (1827m) at the exact foot of the S ridge. Go up grass and stones E into the corridor marking this col (1h15).

Ascend E round steep base of ridge and circle round a hillock 1911m, N and NW, with a little path into a gully. Cross this and traverse up L towards the ribbed crest line. A section of 100m twisting up these ribs and intermediate little gullies in steep rock (I+) relents at a shoulder. Continue just on L(W) side of crest, narrow and airy in places, to a short step (2188m) followed by a pleasant regular ascent on rocks and grass to the summit (1h45; 4h45 from Coche parking). Descend by N ridge.

Parties coming from Gresse and wanting to traverse the mountain via S ridge must cross Pas de la Ville and, 10 min down the W side, turn off L at a cairn (1775m) along a clear little path traversing off SW into the dwarf forest. This joins GR91 some 200m N of the Serrons site; then as for the Coche route (Gresse roadhead to summit, 5h30).

Another approach is feasible from a sharp elbow bend in D8a road between La Bâtie and Les Pellas hamlets N of Mont Aiguille. Drive up forest lane WSW to fork with picnic site pt.1213, whence Pas des Bachassons may be reached by path heading W, to link up with route (see below) coming from Col de Rousset (from pt.1213 to summit, 5h15).

Top: But Sapiau headland from pt. 1382, above Col de Rousset.
Bottom: Planboard of ski area at Col de Rousset.

COL DE ROUSSET   1254m

Saddle proper, 1367m. This summer and winter location on the D518, where the saddle is pierced by a road tunnel which divides the Isère and Drôme departments, has defied the economic vicissitudes of the region by reporting a bouyant number of visitors in both seasons for some years. All services are provided at the E (= N end) of the tunnel. 2 hotels, restaurants, self-catering apartments, dormitory hut, small shop, tourist office, ski-school, chairlift, infrequent bus from La Chapelle and Die. Road on S side from Die (22km) reveals one of the finest and most inviting prospects of the region – steep woodland, bare precipice and limestone pinnacle, tier upon tier, right up to the skyline. At tunnel entrance, a layby enables a retrospective glance to be gained over the heaving Drôme landscape, with Montagne de Glandasse occupying pride of place to the SE.

BUT SAPIAU   1619m

The most frequented headland above Col de Rousset; most of the height can be gained by using the chairlift (normally operates in summer, mid June-end September). From the top of chairlift (1495m) follow broad track, joining GR93, in a gently inclined pasture running up to edge of escarpment ahead; move R to top; plunging depths below, 30 min. All the way from bottom, 1h15.

BUT DE NÈVE   1656m

An easy outing that commands the best views of the Vercors eastern and central plateaux. Starting either from Col de Rousset services (1) at E end of tunnel on the D518 road; or from W end (2), parking on stones.

(1) At rear of platform go up a track in grassy hollow to GR93 path descending from E; follow latter NW in a rising traverse to the physical Col de Rousset (1367m, 30 min). (2) Coming from W end of tunnel, go up GR93 (signpost) in stones to col (20min). From the col follow a path N, edging a wood, for 300m to a clearing; now ignore path. Turn L(W) up clearing to broad grassy shoulder pt.1461. Move up L over 2 narrow limestone ribbons and reach crest. The regular steepness ends abruptly on level summit (about 1h30 from parking places). A descent can be made by the R(N) flank of the SW spur, steep and rough at first, down to the slight Col de Chironne (1416m), where GR93 leads S skirting limestone pavé, then NE along a parapet, back to W end of tunnel (1h down, 1h45 in ascent).

Central section of high Vercors plateau, looking towards inward (W) side of E escarpment. Pt. 2097 = Sommet de Malaval, Pt. 1925 = Pas de la Ville.

Grand Veymont W side, seen across the high Vercors plateau from near pt..1640 (Col de Rousset route).

BUT ST-GENIX 1643m

Great forested headland at S end of Vercors central plateau, and noted regional viewpoint. From the Plainet fountain picnic site (1335m), at a sharp bend in the forestry road system on NE side of the hill, and about 9km S of Vassieux. Follow a track SW over the clearing and go up a trough in the forest to where the track turns sharp R (NNE) at 1410m. Here, a path mounts gently SE in the forest for 250m distance to reach the escarpment/E ridge at Col de la Chau (1431m). Follow small path SW along wooded crest to the open summit slopes, large cairn (1h30).

Access to Grand Veymont S ridge from Col de Rousset

Long, easy and rewarding approach; rates as one of the best excursions in Vercors. From top of chairlift go up to just below But Sapiau headland (1619m); see above. Follow path E on N side of ridge escarpment, no waymarks, up and down grass to the minor Pas de l'Echelette. Do not ascend the steeper slope ahead towards pt.1704. Take path contouring L on N flank and coming to a little rocky trough leading out on to a saddle where a ski track arrives from Chalet des Ours, and just S of pt.1640; large distinctive cairn (much photographed) and tremendous view over the Vercors plateaux (1h). (From Col de Rousset this point may also be reached in 1h from a roadhead used for winter skiing on Montagne de Beurre (1390m), ample parking space. From there follow a track S and SE, passing close to Chalet des Ours and rising ESE to aforementioned saddle).

Follow a path E, descending gradually across grassy slopes for one km into the hollow of Pas des Econdus (1546m). Beyond, and crossing N-S tracks, the path contours below a wood, then ascends ESE for 2km in a broad trough and across limestone pavé with dwarf pines to reach, by going round a rib and down a bowl, the Pré Peyret barn/hut (1595m) under the N side of knoll 1655m (1h15, 2h15 from chairlift or roadhead; 7km).

A barn (1631m) on S side of knoll, which served as the regular overnight halting place, burnt down in the 1980s and has not yet been restored. Note that the water source 130m to the S, by knoll, called Endettés fountain, may be dry, so water should be carried to the barn.

From barn follow path E in a grassy slot for 300m to a large multi coloured cairn and signboard at junction of GR91/93. Quit the GR path and contour SE/ENE round hillock 1654, to enter the Queyrie trough, a long geological fault in the limestone beds which contains a number of interesting features. A little path NE follows grassy stretches in the bed, passes below the Graille

58

SSE

1692

NNW

1685   1706

Font d'Urle (top, at extreme L, centre) and background of Serre de Montué ridge.

headland (1885m, fine regional viewpoint) and ascends to a plain with a few monolith rocks on L - the remains and site of a Roman stone quarry; a little further is a singular blighted tree. Continue on L(NW) side of bed, under Roc Mazilier (1949m), to an incut edge marking the Pas des Bachassons (c1930m). Keep L and head N, going down to pass the Aiguillettes shack on your L. Go on straightahead(N), passing the Pas de Chattons gap (1827m) on your L, and join path curving NW round knoll 1911m to enter and cross the gully giving access to S ridge (qv) of the Grand Veymont (1h30; from Pré Peyret to summit, 3h15; from chairlift, 5h30).

La Chapelle-en-Vercors 900m Large village and an ideal centre for trekking. All main services, 4 hotels, several gîtes within 1-2km, and a lot of B & B type accommodation; 2 campsites, tourist office (75.48.22.54). Public transport in most directions. Little of historic interest; the church is 13th century and nearby will be seen the Cour des Fusillés where some unfortunate hostages were shot by the Nazis in 1944. In winter, nearby Col de Carri has considerable cross-country potential; downhill skiing at Font d'Urle and Col de Rousset - a short drive away.

SERRE DE MONTUÉ 1706m

From Font d'Urle 1435m. A restful early summer walk along a grassy ridge of gently sloping N-S oriented hills; the highest ground in SW Vercors and a highly visible landmark from most of the chief summits of the region. Taxi only from La Chapelle to Font d'Urle; large parking area for cars, as this is primarily a winter skiing centre. In summer, small hotel/restaurant and gîte; gîte has a self-catering apartment, key at a chalet in centre of resort. Access to Font d'Urle from La Chapelle-en-Vercors via D178 to crossroads at the war victims cemetery just short of Vassieux; turn W up to Col de la Chau, then through the thick coniferous Lente forest to an intersection with skitow just visible heading WNW through trees. Turn L(S) along D76b to reach Font d'Urle in a couple of min. Though situated in a sheltered hollow, high winds here in winter make for indifferent snowcover for local skiers. If it looks a bit of a one-horse place, there are literally dozens of horses in summer grazing on nearby hillsides; a reminder that this is also a centre for cross-country riding.

For the hill walk, leave the gîte and go about 200m N along road towards chalets and pick up GR93 (poorly marked) as it snakes up the first short slope. Then steer WSW, later WNW up grassy slopes towards Pas de l'Infernet. Better views now obtained

60

of Font d'Urle, revealing that it has rearward slopes that tilt gently up to Port d'Urle and other features along a smooth ridge, rimmed with cliffs on the far side, above an immense cirque overlooking St-Julien-en-Quint. Leaving pt.1658 well to L, the path approaches though avoids the next top (1698m) on ridge as it passes a shepherds' hut. It then heads NNW for Pas de l'Infernet (some feeble fencing on edge of sheer drops into cirque) to circumvent pt.1692 by a little col. From here, a well trodden path along main Serre de Montué ridge stretches N. Traverse next summit on ridge; the path skirts it halfway up on W side; so pt. 1706 is finally attained. The height marked on its cairn is wrong. Views W to Col de la Bataille and Rhône valley. In the immediate foreground, mainly deciduous forest is seen on W slopes, at some places reaching to within 50m of ridge.

Return to resort by a contouring path along E slopes in an ideal leisurely descent. No drinking water in evidence; unpromising drinking-troughs seen on the way down are obviously designed for quadrupeds (2h30-3h for round trip).

Placard advising visitors of the regulations and dangers applying to the high Vercors plateau.

TRIÈVES

A relatively large area of gentle hills, precipices and shallow valleys S of Grenoble, skirted by roads to Sisteron. Wedged between the Vercors and Dévoluy to the SW and SE respectively, with the Matheysine hills and Drac valley as its N border, Trièves is a kind of climatic halfway house between Mediterranean climes to the S, and the alpine rigours of High Dauphiné. With mean altitudes hovering above the 700m mark, the air hereabouts, so they say, is the purest in France. What with dry summers – Mens has only 857mm of rain for a total of 93 days per year – but plentiful rainfall on the periphery (Tréminis has 1107mm of rain in 108 days), and several streams converging on the Ebron torrent fed by the snows of Grand Ferrand, the area has proved suitable for human habitation since the earliest times.

Up to the end of the Middle Ages a major trade route from Provence used to cross the district, passing through Mens, its chief town, fording the Drac and climbing to La Mure. The surrounding pastures were also much frequented by transhumants from the Basses-Alpes. Trièves itself concentrated on sheep-rearing and its vineyards used to produce a rough little wine till the 1950s, now discontinued. In recent times wheat growing and cattle breeding have become bread-winners. However, shunned by railway and main road alike, Trièves has a relaxed, sleepy atmosphere, as if the world had passed it by – which explains why many a Grenoblois has a second house in the area. The controversial Grenoble-Sisteron motorway proposal, if and when it is adopted, is likely to change the secluded world that some enjoy at present.

Modern developments notwithstanding, the quiet romantic charm of Trièves will not be lost on the visitor. It has several outstanding churches, some in the inimitable 13th century Romance style (Mens, Prébois, etc). Mens has a Protestant church, a reminder that Trièves was a bone of contention in the religious wars. Since then, the French novelist Giono and the landscape painter Edith Berger have found inspiration in the peaceful rural scenes and harmonious natural environment.

Mountain walkers can adopt either Chichilianne, Clelles, Mens or Tréminis as a base for excursions into the surroundings. Wide variety of accommodation to suit most pockets, including Gîte de France furnished chalets, and camping grounds with alternative convivial *camping à la ferme* formula. At the foot of Mt Aiguille is Château de Passières, a classy little hotel with gourmet cuisine to celebrate a successful climb (76.34.45.48). The cheaper and friendly Au Gai Soleil du Mont Aiguille (76.34.41.71) with traditional Trièves cooking may suit others. Try the local cheese (Carre du Trièves) and raviole. Mens (pronounced Maanse = thin) has just one hotel; recommended is excellent food at Le Passé Simple café-restaurant (76.34.65.35); tourist office (76.34.65.67). Tréminis has camping facilities, also gîte/refuge accommodation; for latter see Christian Zanardi at Tréminis-L'Eglise (76.34.71.96).

ROC DE PEYROLE 2016m

Via Pas de l'Aiguille and the S Vercors plateau, a relatively long though easy undertaking to reach N summit of the Glandasse escarpment overlooking Die. **Chichilianne** is the nearest bus access pt.(in full view of Mont Aiguille to N); hotel, gîte, taxi hire. With a car, drive to La Richardière, parking at roadhead (1057m) beyond this hamlet; 4km from Chichilianne (taxi).

Follow a gently sloping track WSW to large clearing with a war memorial. At end of this clearing a path enters undergrowth and commences a gradual ascending traverse, later becoming steeper with zags and risk of stonefall as the Pas de l'Aiguille is approached. Residual snow here quite late in season (May); cross in memory of WW2 resistance fighters; good view of Mont Aiguille, resembling the prow of a large vessel in distance, hence its nickname *le Grand Navire* (1h45 from Richardière).

From Pas de l'Aiguille (1622m) follow a depression due S to the Chaumailloux hut on edge of grassy Vercors plateau (1669m). Head W for some 500m before bearing SW in direction of Roc Peyrole now visible in the distance. This well marked path, also used by pony trekkers passes Jasneuf sheep-pen (1627m) and carries on SW across Plaine de la Gache to a major intersection with GR91/93, the Quatre Chemins du Jasneuf (1h30 from Pas). Now keep to GR91 as it heads SW to Jas de la Ville, then steer S to ascend slopes leading to pt.1906 (1h). Leave the GR and work SW to reach edge of escarpment, whence Roc de Peyrole is soon reached. Broad vistas over the Diois region (30-45 min; about 5h from roadhead outside La Richardière). Return by same route.

See under excursions in Diois for another route to this Glandasse summit.

MONT AIGUILLE 2087m

The most striking landmark in the whole of this guidebook area and a prominent feature in views for anyone journeying from Grenoble to Lus-la-Croix-Haute. A dramatic rock fortress that became separated over the centuries from the main Urgonian limestone pavé of the Vercors plateau. A lodestone that attracts both climbers and ramblers. Nothing is more remarkable about this singular elongated tower - whose name appears as *mons inascensibilis* in writings from the 10th century onwards - than the time and circumstances of its first ascent.

In 1492 - the year that Columbus discovered America - Antoine de Ville, as Julien de Beaupré, lord of Montélimar and Saoû, and Chamberlain to the King, by order of Charles VIII of France and in order to comply with what (at that period at any rate) must have seemed a remarkable whim on the part of the monarch, ascended on 26 June the Eguille Fort or, as it was called locally, Mont Inaccessible (its other local name, Mont Agulle, slightly transformed, is the one that has survived). De Ville, who was accompanied by 7 followers, made careful preparations and conducted several reconnaissances before effecting the ascent with the aid of ropes, ladders and masonry tools. The latter can be assumed to be 15th century equivalents of today's equipment for artificial climbing, while De Ville was also the King's expert on storming castle walls.

They remained on top for a week, long enough to receive official acknowledgement of their feat from the Grenoble parliament while onlookers below watched their activities, or joined them on the summit. François de Bosco, almoner to De Ville, related how they found a lovely meadow and a fine group of chamois which he said could never leave the summit. This flight of fancy contrasts with the observation of wild sparrows mottled red, black and grey, ravens with red feet (probably choughs) and other extraordinary unknown birds, as well as beautiful flowers, some of unexplained kind. The party built some huts, and, in keeping with religious zeal of the times, planted 3 crosses - one on each of the 3 highest points. Further comments were made on enduring the "horrible descent". There is speculation over whether or not a local shepherd, named Jaime, guided them to the summit; the actual route followed is also speculative although now generally believed to have been the Tubulaires, and not the Voie Normale of today.

The documents which certify this ascent are preserved in the Isère Place de Verdun archives at Grenoble. Coolidge reproduced

Mont Aiguille SE face.

them in his monumental work about Josias Simler published in Grenoble, 1904.

Mont Aiguille had to wait 350 years for another ascent, supposedly made on 16 June 1834 by Joseph Thiollier, curé of Chichilianne, and Eugène Rochas, a lawyer from Gap, accompanied by local men including a Jean Liotard. The party had the full paraphernalia of ropes, ladders and masons' hammers. According to another version Liotard did it alone, shouting all the time to watchers below. On reaching the top, "after considerable difficulties", an idyllic meadow was found but no animals, living or dead. On the highest point a fragment of wall remained of a hut assumed built in 1492, while the crosses had collapsed. As to traces of De Ville's artificial aids, they had disappeared, no doubt in the 17th century, when a mammoth rockfall sliced away a chunk of the NW corner of the mountain. Since then the 1834 ascent has been disputed and it is now generally regarded as a fiction.

There came a series of further successful attempts by locals. On 28 July 1849, 3 lads from Gresse, called Cotte, Moutet and Paturel made it to the top, leaving a small iron cross with their names inscribed. They were allegedly followed by Liotard's son in 1853, and by a man from Clelles in 1864. In 1875, a local railway engineer working on the new Grenoble-Gap line, called Desfilhes, got to the top with a certain Rigobert Magadon from Clelles. It was also in Magadon's company that the first properly recorded tourist ascent was made by Edouard Rochat, a well respected explorer, on 17 September 1877. A variation story related to this ascent states that one A. Maurice, a local man who claimed to have been up already in 1875, also accompanied Rochat.

Rochat's 'first' by a 'monchu', or city-bred gentleman, set the trend for mountain climbing in the area at a time when the Grenoble section of the CAF was showing interest in Mont Aiguille. They had in situ pegs and chains installed on the ordinary route between 1878-1880 by Magadon, ever willing to oblige. Thus was one of the first ever 'via ferrata' set up in the Alps.

W A B Coolidge with Emmanuel Ferrat son, 29 August 1881 discovered an extensive sloping grassy meadow, many flowers, at least one stunted pine tree and the cross planted in 1849. But mercenary Coolidge thought the fee of 25 francs asked by his young guide rather high, though later modified this view "for the well-hidden and intricate way which has yet been discovered to the summit of this freak of nature".

A controversial first 'guideless' climb was made by E Thorant and party on 14 June 1891. Thorant later went on to make a first

66

ascent on the N face with H Chaumat on 25 August 1895. First (modern) ascent of Tubulaires route: M Lughinbühl, L Zvingelstein, 4 June 1922. Since 1950 some 2 dozen climbs have been put up on various facets of the rock, seldom below grade IV and mostly V or VI. Other firsts include landings by a pair of Sikorsky helicopters on the summit meadow, 25 August 1957, followed 2 days later by H Giraud with a Piper Cub. Stunts of this kind continued till 1960 when they were banned by the local authority. A new 'via ferrata' was installed in 1990 so the hoi polloi could get up. Considered unethical by true alpinists, it was dismantled within a year by a commando of purists. Finally on 27 January 1992 extreme-skiers P Tardivel and R Lécluse skied down the W face via Tubulaires ! This was done with some abseiling, but where and when exactly is not stated. What was to have been the 500th anniversary of De Ville's historic climb, over the 27–28 June 1992 weekend, proved a total washout due to bad weather.

Normal Route on WNW face. Called the Entonnoir, or des Cables. Grade II/II+. Proper boots, helmet and rope essential. From La Richardière (1022m) go up well marked path N to Col de l'Aupet (1627m). From N side of col traverse with a small path to R(E) through pines and over scree for a few min. to start of climb at foot of steep rock; iron ring in rock and paint (2h-2h15).

Follow a first ledge L, then cross a gully on R and climb a chimney, narrow at top, leading to small terrace. Follow on to three chimneys; take R-hand one. Emerging from this, move R(W) and go down to first cable. Traverse along a narrow level ledge running L-R towards deep cleft that separates the Vierge tower from the main wall. Now attain the Entonnoir by crossing a polished sloping slab (cable), circumventing a hump-backed step to cross the cleft, then backing down across a short wall (cable) into the Entonnoir. Due to frequent stonefall, not a good place to linger.

Now reach and cross upper part of scree slope that occupies lower portion of the Entonnoir. Go up a small chimney on L to reach bottom of Entonnoir proper. Climb in middle of the wall opposite to a ledge which is followed for a few m R(S). Scale another short wall to second ledge. To its L is a curious feature, Passage des Meules - a series of flat millstone-like slabs, between which the climber has to stoop to pass (15m, cable). Then a few m along ledge to the final chimney.

This chimney angles up at about 50°, with 4 overhanging steps to negotiate en route. A bit tricky at times but the cable (a double-edged weapon, as it also dislodges stones !) is there to help. After 4th step the chimney opens out and summit plateau (650m x 100m) is soon reached, whence a few min. walk across slope to summit at NE end (1h15-1h45 from bottom).

Warning: temptation for youngsters to slide down grass on their backsides should be resisted as there have been fatalities. The rockface in the vicinity of the Normal Route is 250m high.

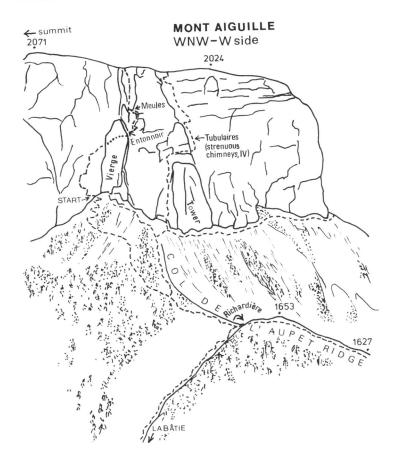

MONT AIGUILLE
WNW–W side

TÊTE CHEVALIÈRE 1951m

A fairly remarkable feature that towers high above Chichilianne and a worthwhile vantage point. Easily reached from La Richardière via the Pas de l'Aiguille as described under Roc de Peyrole (above). From the hut just S of the Pas, a path runs generally SE. It passes a spring, Source de Chevalière, and contours N side of the Tête des Baumiers knoll (1874m), to resume a SE course. After intersection with a side path heading S (ignore), continue for about 500m before leaving path near Bergerie de Chamousset to strike NE across gently sloping limestone pavé that leads without problems to summit. Several deep clefts in pavé may hold snow to late in season (about 3h15 from La Richardière roadhead).

A circuit is possible for descending to Chichilianne via a path that follows rim SE to Pas de l'Essaure (1714m), then zigzags steeply down through forest to village (2h from summit; 5h15 for round trip).

Essaure – Col de Menée ridge traverse

Rewarding though energetic circuit for a Chichilianne based party, provided someone (or taxi by arrangement) is prepared to collect party on arrival at Col de Menée.

From gîte d'étape in Chichilianne take upper road ESE and in 400m go into first lane on R; it becomes a path heading SW. This climbs steeply S up Combe du Four into forest, crosses Ruisseau des Arches and winds up SW to Pas de l'Essaure c1670m (1h30). Head due S to Refuge de l'Essaure (1653m, 30 min). Follow on SE along path to reach sheep-pen 500m further on. Continue in same direction along a track down to the Fontaine des Prêtres (1456m); picnic site at top of Combau farm track.

Now reascend slopes SE to reach pt.1714 on the Crête de Grande Leirie which yields simple ridge wandering with stupendous views over Trièves. Appreciate contrast between vigorously forested green slopes to NE and bare drier country to S. After La Sistreire (1635m) go down to Col de Menée, 1457m (2h from Essaure hut, 4h from Chichilianne). Spacious parking areas at both ends of Menée tunnel; undoubtedly one of the finest beauty spots in S Vercors. Return N to Chichilianne by a road winding through magnificent forest.

Col de Menée 1457m

Name is derived from the word *minuit* (midnight) and recalls the troubled times of the religious wars when Protestants, persecuted

69

in Die, used to flee by way of this pass to reach the relatively safe haven of Mens. Midnight was the time for these fugitives to try their luck, as the sentry on duty at the guardpost on the pass was usually asleep by then.

In winter 2 skitows on the S slopes of La Sistreire (1635m) cater for local Trièves and Diois skiers. The best time for a visit is undoubtedly May/June when the pastures are covered with lush grass and the beech trees are a vivid green; the contrast between the pre-Mediterranean atmosphere of the adret slopes, and the cool shade of the ubac is truly startling. The col is also a jump-off point for further endeavours in a SE direction.

Above the col, working ESE along the ridge, now through woodland, now crossing meadows, one may reach **Mont Barral** (1903m) with no difficulty in 1h30. Along the fine ridge S of Barral, the path is joined by GR93 near pt.1774m (Crête de Jaboui), and this ridge can be continued at length over La Roberche (1853m) and Col de Seysse to the Jocou (2051m, qv; 2h30). Descending S for an hour or so enables the hamlet of Grimone to be reached (gîte).

– o –

L' AIGUILLE (DE L'OBIOU)   2037m

A Trièves classic for a Mens based party, along an interesting portion of the Tour de l'Obiou circuit path, and in a decidedly alpine setting. Impressive close-up views unfold of the Grande Tête de l'Obiou (2789m). Early summer/autumn outing; proper boots and ski-pole or similar useful; not to be attempted with snow cover, as traverse to Col de l'Aiguille can then prove troublesome. From Mens drive (or take a taxi) along D66/216 to St-Baudille-et-Pipet (handsome church) and to intersection beyond (880m). Leave the D216 Tréminis road and turn off along side road D216b towards Longueville. Arresting views R to steep forested slopes giving way higher up to huge cirques and rugged arêtes. In 2km, just before Longueville at a bend (1001m), a track forks R (E) with 2 different signposts marked: Rochassac. About 200m of track leads to a large clearing by the Vanne torrent; parking is possible here on gravel.

Cross torrent by plank bridge and head up path now converted into track by 4WD logging tractors. Profusion of rose-hip in early stages to cableway station (used by transhumants at the Rochassac sheep-pen). Cross Pierre Aigue streambed (usually dry) and soon start a prolonged backbreaker up steep wooded slopes bearing SE. Eventually reach a brow and turn L(E). After

100m, a recent 4WD variation on L is ignored. Go on up brow for another 200m or so when the bona fide path will be discovered slanting off through the forest at a low angle to the L (blue waymarks; just a few stripes, mostly small triangles on trees). In the shade of this essentially coniferous forest, with boxwood undergrowth, following the zigzags of this carefully made path is pure joy. Thus to head of the forest, with spectacular views L and R to adjoining cirques; all of it very broken terrain with rockbands and precipices. Rather more deciduous trees now; the path is stonier as it makes short zags to circumvent a waterfall or limestone outcrop. Trees full of birds (titmice, woodpecker, firecrest, etc). Gradually veering L to R, path outflanks a rock band guarding access to the Rochassac meadows, and soft, dewy grass is found underfoot. A few zags later the CAF Rochassac hut (1688m) is reached (1h45).

This hut consists of 2 buildings: a ramshackle part sporting the CAF plaque (locked, key obtainable at Mens, phone 76.34.61.77), and a more recent structure (c1987) with first floor, also locked and marked: Refuge. Some broken chairs and benches outside, together with a large wooden kennel (sheepdog?). Fresh spring water is the only redeeming feature of what used to be a much frequented refuge, originally assembled in the 1950s with parts flown in by helicopter, and the site then of an annual ski trophy on the agreeably steep adjacent slopes; this was a time when most ski enthusiasts were still mountaineers and hadn't forgotten how to walk!

Head N a short way up grassy slope to a sheep-pen (1725m); look out for the red/green Tour de l'Obiou flashes on rocks. A visible trod makes off NNE past 2 deciduous trees in an ascending traverse of the Rochassac meadows; one sharp turn SE brings us to the Tour de l'Obiou footpath. Follow this as it contours N to attain Col de l'Aiguille (1966m). Initially the terrain is straightforward on grass. Before col, however, the path skirts head of 2 gullies and the resultant erosion and loose scree necessitate extreme caution. In mid-June conditions the writer had only the hoof marks of chamois to guide him through; by end of summer, after a lot of feet have scraped the ground, the path line should be easier to follow. From the col a gentle grassy flower-studded incline mounts N to summit in a few min. Interesting views to Rattier, Bonnet de l'Evêque and other features of the Obiou group (1h15, 3h from Vanne torrent parking).

Returning by the same route, pay particular attention to tricky scree section under the col (1h45 back to Vanne torrent, allow 5h for round trip).

Top: Aiguille de l'Obiou and Col de l'Aiguille, showing last stretch of path to
Bottom: Old CAF Rochassac hut on way to Aiguille de l'Obiou.

MÉNIL (MÉNIS) 1594m

Conspicuous wooded pyramid commanding entrance to the Tréminis cirque, well worth a visit if only for extensive views afforded of the continuous W wall of Dévoluy, of which it constitutes an outlying spur.

Access from the N75 at the Lalley turn-off, 4km N of Croix-Haute pass, then by D66 and D216 to Tréminis (community bus, gîte, etc). Carry on N up narrow winding road beneath eroded precipices of Les Echarennes to Mens col (1111m), a wild-looking place with forests of pine and fir all round. Park vehicle on the roadside near col.

Take broad forest track heading W along ridge. Signpost here states: Ménis 1h30. Blue waymarks and other indications occur at irregular intervals all the way to summit. Some 100m from the start ignore a small path slipping L downhill, signposted: Tréminis. A little further on likewise ignore grassy path to L. Forest track now steepens noticeably, levelling out again after 200m. After pt.1268 it heads on up and across N slopes of mountain to the R. Do not follow it; turn L at signpost marked: Ménil, and head SW along an excellent path, slightly exposed in one or two places, that makes a gentle ascending traverse through fir and boxwood, working round the S ridge, to emerge on W flank of the mountain. Initially, there are challenging views L(SE) through the firs to Grand Ferrand, later replaced by propects of Jocou and the S Trièves, till one is virtually on the N side.

At an intersection leave path to L (signpost: Le Moulin), and go R to commence a series of zigzags with path a bit exposed at first atop steep slopes. Work slowly back to the R(SE) through mixed forest, to emerge on steep open grassy slopes ending at the summit ridge. All round view of Trièves, Dévoluy, Matheysine and Vercors (1h30-1h45 from Mens col). Ideal outing for early spring when higher ground in area is still under snow.

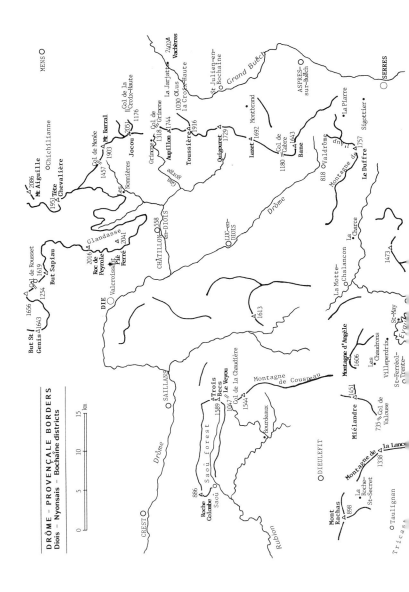

DRÔME – PROVENÇAL BORDERS
Diois – Nyonsais – Bochaîne districts

0   5   10   15
km

MENS ○

○Chichilianne

Chichilianne

△2096
Mt Aiguille
Tête 1951△
Chevalière

Col de Menée
1457

Col de la
Croix-Haute
1176

2402△
Vachères

Grand Buëch

△Mt Barral
1903

Nonnières ●
Les

Jocou 2051△

Col de
Grimone
1318

La Jarjatte
1090 ○Lus
la Croix-Haute

St Julien-en-
○Bochaîne

ASPRES-
sur-Buëch ○

○ SERRES

Col de
Grimone
1318 Grimone○

Aupillon△1744

Toussière△
1916

Quiguret△
1729

Luzet△
1692

Montbrand
●

La Piarre
●

Sigottier ●

Glandasse

But St
Genis△1643
1656

Col de Rousset
1254 1619△

But Sapiau

Roc de Peyrole
2016△

Saint-
Plé
Perré 2041

Valcroissant ●

CHÂTILLON-
en-DIOIS ○ 558

○LUC-en-
DIOIS

Drôme

Col de
Cabre
1180 1643
Bane

Montagne de △1757
Le Duffre

818 ○Valdrôme

Montagne de Durvil

DIE ○

SAILLANS ○

Drôme

Saoû forest

△Trois
Becs
1589 1047// Le Veyou
1544

Col de la Chaudière

Montagne de Cousteau

1613

La Motte-
○Chalancon

La
Charce

1472

St-May ●
Eygal

Montagne d'Angèle
606

Les
Chaudrons ●
Villeperdrix●
St-Ferréol-
○ Trente-

CREST ○

Drôme

Roche
Colombe
886

Saoû ●

Bourdeaux ●

Miélandre
△1451

Col de
Valouse
735

○DIEULEFIT

Mont
Rachas
898△

La
Roche-
St-Secret ●

Montagne de △ la Lance
1338

Tricasa
● Taulignan

Rubion

DIOIS

Quite a large natural region of the Dauphiné Pré-Alps, drained by the river Drôme and its principal tributaries. It has a pleasantly dry Mediterranean climate with only 90mm of rain per year in Die, the chief town, while on at least 80 days a year the temperature drops below 0°C. Average altitudes are lower than in Vercors and few hills S of the Drôme exceed 1500m, with the highest tops in the Lus Aiguilles (2400m) to the E. Tectonically speaking things become somewhat complicated with an intertwining system of N-S ridges, and sheltered valleys trapped in the all-enclosing generally steep limestone slopes of some basin of syncline (Saoû, Charens, Valdrôme, etc). On ubac slopes one finds pine, occasionally beech, together with residual clumps of fir (Trois Becs, Duffre, etc), pubescent oak, thyme and Mediterranean-style heath appearing on adret slopes and valley floors.

Although much depleted by rural exodus - population density reduced to 3 inhabitants per sq.km in the countryside - traditional activities such as agriculture (grapes, barley and to a lesser extent, wheat) and animal husbandry have managed to survive. Though cattle are few in number, sheep are bred over most of the area. Belonging to the hardy Pré-Alps stock they give a comparatively high yield, being well adapted to extensive, semi-arid and slightly prickly local pastures. They also tend to be more respectful of trees and shrubs than goats, which are on the increase, while pigs are also raised. The Die slaughterhouse processes some 500 tons of mutton a year; the town also also plays host every June to a crowd-puller and photo occasion called *La fête de la transhumance,* when droves of sheep invade the streets.

The Diois region, however, is chiefly remarkable for the all-pervading institution of **clairette de Die,** as the locally produced sparkling wine is called. But beware wine-buffs. Swanky roadside places with razzle-dazzle names and spacious carparks try to persuade with a lot of hot air about grape-picking and fermentation before selling bottles of the stuff with a fancy cuvée tradition label. You can obtain the same vintage more cheaply at La-Chapelle-en-Vercors, let alone an even cheaper price in any Grenoble supermarket! Nevertheless it is superb bubbly with a very grapey taste. Production goes back to Roman times. No less an authority than Pliny the Elder lavished praise on the

Dea Augusta wine in AD77. In 1942 it was granted AOC status and now comes in *brut* and *demi-sec* denominations. Some people debase their **clairette** by adding cassis, but the wine should be savoured on its own if its flavour is to be fully appreciated. It is produced on both sides of the Drôme valley, but some of the choicest locations are on sunny S-facing slopes between Die and Châtillon. The Combemare vineyards situated at 600m, below the Glandasse cliffs, are the highest in France. Châtillon also also produces a perfectly acceptable red wine, the *Cuvée du Parc,* while a non-sparkling dry white is also obtainable locally.

SAOÛ FOREST

The finest basin of syncline and least spoiled beauty spot in the area is rather like a thickly wooded, miniature Vercors. Imagine a bathtub 12.5km long and 2-2.5km wide, the sides of which are in fact a rampart of limestone cliffs from Roche Colombe (886m) in the W to Veyou (1589m), highest of the imposing Trois Becs group, in the E, just above the Chaudière col (1047m). Beyond the last named feature lies the long Couspeau ridge, unremarkable except as a venue for para-gliders.

Two roads lead into this secluded haven: one from the Drôme valley to the N, via Pas de Lauzens; the other from picturesque Saoû village by means of narrow Le Pertuis canyon, through which runs the Vèbre - responsible for draining 90% of entire catchment area and a noted trout stream. In bygone days toddlers used to be dipped in its icy waters as part of a toughening up process. Today the Saoû trout hatcheries (75.76.02.78) are open to the public.

Inside this 'lost valley' drive carefully, watching out for 'sleeping policemen' over some 4km of good metalled road, past stands of beech, fir, oak and pine, interspersed with verdant clearings, along to an improbable roadhead with parking-lot beneath stately cedars, opposite the Auberge des Dauphins (467m), a now abandoned miniature version of the Versailles Trianon. A shady, forested and well-watered location ideal for picnics. No accommodation or refreshments available; adjoining buildings belong to the Forestry Commission. Visitors must therefore make their own arrangements; sleeping in a van is apparently tolerated. **Saoû** village has a hotel, gîte d'étape, B & B house, campsite and a couple of restaurants (Syndicat d'Initiative: 75.76.01.72).

Apart from its scope for rambling and climbing, Saoû is chiefly outstanding as a wildlife reserve. Quadrupeds such as chamois, roe deer, marmot and badger haunt the forest glades, sometimes venturing above the tree-line at daybreak, while 110 species of birds have been recorded here, most remarkable of which are the black woodpecker, great spotted woodpecker, tree creeper, crossbill, Tengmalm's owl, rock thrush, common buzzard, kestrel, snake-eating eagle and golden eagle.

SAOÛ EXCURSIONS

St–Médard Chapel 858m A 2h loop on the Saoû N rim, starting from a forest track that heads N from the Vèbre torrent about 3km W of the Auberge des Dauphins roadhead.

Roche Colombe 886m By car through Le Pertuis, then WNW along D70 to point just short of Pont d'Horta (423m), whence woodland footpath is taken W to Pas de l'Echelette (711m). A traverse of Roche Colombe cliffs (a venue for rock climbers) brings one to Le Maupas, just E of pt. 884; then a descent SE to Saoû village (4h).

Grand Pomerolle 1082m From Auberge des Dauphins roadhead (467m), a 5h loop through forest and along the Saoû S rim; this is a combination of forest tracks, paths and some rougher going, taking in Les Berches (1025m), Grand Pomerolle itself, Pas de Berthe (884m) and Petit Pomerolle (822m). Rock climbing activity hereabouts. Waymarked by 2 thin parallel yellow flashes.

Les Trois Becs

From Auberge des Dauphins roadhead (467m), an ambitious 8h outing. Signpost at start; waymarks of 2 thin parallel yellow flashes. The first part is along flattish wooded ground, following the Vèbre upstream. After pt. 725, track climbs steadily to Virage du Pré de l'Ane (1210m), where the Trois Becs circuit proper starts. Go N via GR9 as it describes 3 or 4 zags towards upper levels of beech forest, bypassing Refuge des Girards (hut), till Roche de la Laveuse (1376m) is attained. Veer SE along the clifftop to Col des Auberts (1395m) for actual N-S traverse of Trois Becs. No real climbing, just plain walking, some of it fairly strenuous, as successively Roche Courbe (1545m), Le Signal (1559m) and Le Veyou (1589m), together with intervening dips, are tackled. Path descends Pré de l'Ane to Pas de Siara (1295m), before linking up with approach route at Virage du Pré de l'Ane.

This trip can be done on mountain bikes, but it probably means carrying machines along rough sections of the main Trois Becs.

[N.B. Starting point for each of the above excursions is indicated by signpost; waymarking is by means of 2 thin parallel yellow flashes].

Le Veyou from Col de la Chaudière.

LE VEYOU 1589m

A remarkable peak, the culminating point of the Trois Becs group. It can be reached quite rapidly from Col de la Chaudière (1074m). Choice of approaches, either from the hospitable village of Bourdeaux, via narrow switchback D156 mounting the SW slopes that have a distinctly sub-arid Provençal look about them. Or, more sedate progress from Saillans in the N, with the gaunt cliffs of Roche Courbe initially seen as a distant backcloth to the famed Clairette de Die vineyards. Coming up in this way, the cliffs acquire majesty and prestige at closer quarters; as you near them they tower impressively above the pinewoods in a setting worthy of a much higher range.

The Roche Courbe cliffs, called locally La Pelle and known to climbers by various sectional names, give hard routes of 250-350m. The original climb was made by a Parisien team in 1961.

Prior to 1990 it was usual to park a car by Siara Farm, just above the col, then follow blue flashes to Pas de Siara. No longer. The farmhouse, suitably restored with well-tended lawns and swimming pool, has now become the hideaway of a privacy-seeker. The property is barricaded in with wire fence and locked gate overlooked by a TV monitor. The former access route is effectively blocked. While freshwater spring and picnic tables have, admittedly, been placed at the public's disposal, *amis randonneurs,* as the new proprietor ambiguously terms them on a prominent **no trespass** notice nearby, are now obliged to circumvent the estate up steep bushy slopes and slippery little ravines. After some 300m of this thoroughly distasteful terrain, intermittent blue flashes appear, now considerably worn, as the path zigzags up a spur. Remain on path, taking care not to venture too far L(S) where debris strewn ledges angle down dangerously into a sheer gully. At head of gully path strikes L (one briefly exposed stride) before commencing mildly ascending traverse above steep drops; it then enters and crosses a strip of beech forest to emerge above tree line and low rockbands onto Pas de Siara (1295m). This is a broad, grassy saddle between Veyou and a similar, slightly lower wooded feature to S. Usually some crows in the vicinity; chamois guaranteed early in the day.

Turn N as path makes a beeline up steep gradient, after a while veering R. It then swings back L as slope relents. Path is well worn - more of a trough, really - with double yellow flashes now observed. Path circles Veyou, revealing vistas of entire forested syncline to the W, with tree line a bare 50m or so below. Veyou summit consists of sub-alpine pasture with a variety of dwarf juniper and gold-splotched with buttercups in spring. Side path

angles up R(E) to the stony top marked by small cairn. Below the actual summit lies a grassy ledge sloping down to edge of main rock face. Views N to the other 2 'becs', visibly lower and easily attainable by path. Return to Col de la Chaudière by the same route; round trip, about 2h15.

– o –

Die 238m pop.4000. Since the early 1960s, when 'Chacal' in Frederick Forsyth's *Day of the Jackal* suppressed a premonitory shudder at the sight of the town's name, no doubt other Britons have been, if not similarly affected, then at least puzzled on entering Die (pronounced Dee). As the walled town of Dea Augusta Vocontiorum, it was already famous as a market place and centre for bull and ram worship in Roman times. With such a long and at times tumultuous history, several vestiges of the past are visible today. The town's ramparts, 11th century cathedral, Protestant church, a museum well stocked with Gallo-Roman and early Christian relics, not to mention a bust of Beatrix of Die, a renowned 13th century poetess, are tourist attractions. Otherwise today the town is a quiet little Drôme sub-prefecture.

Tourism has become one of the chief activities with a strategic location between Vercors and Provence, clement weather and an efficient road network. All main services and many shops; 5 hotels, 2 gîtes, furnished rooms and no fewer than 5 campsites – 4 of them on the banks of the Drôme with bathing facilities; swimming pool, tennis courts and – proof that Provence is not far away – a large ground for *pétanque*. Several pony trekking and horse riding centres; bicycle hire at the Office du Tourisme (75.22.03.03) near the town centre; mountain-bikes from at least 4 agencies. Athletes may take part in the now classic Die – Col de Rousset marathon in May, or in a fell-running contest in Sept.

MONTAGNE DE GLANDASSE 2041m

A somewhat tautological name derived from local patois. Thus Glan = high mountain, asse = massive, for this final S-ward thrusting spur of Vercors whose cliffs entirely dominate Die's easterly prospects. By no means a graceful summit, but undoubtedly a majestic one that may receive fresh dustings of snow well into May when N winds blow. For long a refuge for bears and wolves, Glandasse is now home to eagles and buzzards, chamois and ibex; even more so as numerous transhumants, who used to arrive on foot from Camargue and the Baronnies before 1972, now use lorries to reach more accessible pastures. The herds that do visit in summer still leave plenty of room for wildlife to thrive in peace.

Although an attraction for rock climbers, Glandasse may be scaled by mountain walkers. (See under Trièves for a route from the N). At least 4 footpaths wend a way up the W slopes; 2 are described below; both should be treated with respect in the wet, especially the acrobatic descent into the cirque between Col des Bachassons (1661m) and Rochers des Traverses (1781m).

Pié Ferré 2041m Chief summit of Glandasse. The approach from Châtillon-en-Diois (14km SE of Die) is the easiest way and uses GR91 for most of the ascent. From Châtillon (570m) follow the footpath winding up N through steep woods; towards the end of this long climb it circumvents an impressive spur, Saut de l'Ane (1463m = donkey's leap), then zigzags up to a plateau to reach the Châtillon huts (1758m, 3h45). From here one can peer down into the spectacular Cirque de l'Archiane (qv). The GR is now followed across flattish ground in a general NW direction to go round Pié Ferré (or Le Dôme). Leave path and work up steeply L(W) to attain culminating point (1h, about 4h45 all told). GR91 can be continued N to the main Vercors plateau and the Trièves district so reached.

Roc de Peyrole 2016m Leaving Die by N93, turn L at pt.408 along a small road SE, up past Sallières (pony trekking, etc) to Valcroissant Abbey (649m). This 12th century Cistercian relic may be visited if permission is obtained (phone 75.22.12.70).

Follow path E from Valcroissant up grassy slope into forest; keep to L side of dry streambed. Path makes 5 zags to reach the Sentier du Tour du Glandasse. Turn L(N) along this for some 800m to intersection (1021m) where R-hand path is taken. Continue up through forest bearing initially SE past Fontaine de Juillet (spring), then trending S and, after a while, passing near some stones on R of path referred to as Pierres de Sacrifice (c1200m). The slope now steepens and path swings L(E); it quits the forest and zigzags up grassy slopes interspersed with trees to La Pale, where another path comes in from Serre de Cologne to the S. The main path winds up grass/stone slopes to ruins named Malcollet (1855m) on a prominent platform (4h15 from Valcroissant).

Now follow GR91 N to Laval d'Aix sheep-pen; then steer W before returning N to circumvent a double summit (1966m). As soon as GR91 has finished rounding W spur of latter summit, leave it and follow N a trod that passes between a deep hollow (La Courouane) and a tabular feature. Then bear L (NW) up steep slope to top of Roc de Peyrole (1h30, 5h45 from Valcroissant).

Châtillon-en-Diois 570m Superby situated at the foot of Gland-asse. The name is merely that of its now ruined medieval castle, and the same atmosphere is retained as one strolls through narrow alley-ways known as 'viols' in the centre. An excellent excursion base at the intersection of 3 GR footpaths while Archiane, Col de Menée and Grimone are rapidly attainable by car/taxi.

This pleasantly tidy village with plenty of fountains and shade is much sought after by tent dwellers, for whom there is a fine camping ground by the river. Services include several hotels and restaurants, groceries and other shops. Wine cellars offer *clairette* and local red and rosé wines. Bus shuttle 'Transdrôme' runs from Die station to Châtillon.

In the neighbourhood sporting activities include mini-golf, white water canoeing, mountain biking (for latter, and hire, contact Aloa on 75.21.13.63) and horse riding with Dominique Malassagne (75.21.17.99). Ordinary bikes for hire some 10km along D69 at Luc-en-Diois (75.21.34.14). Gourmets should go on the Train des Vignes excursion - a little train that visits Châtillon's vine-yards after a slap-up meal in a local restaurant with *caillette du Diois* and a half *coquelet à la Clairette de Die* on the menu (advanced bookings possible, 75.44.36.30).

Cirque de l'Archiane

Recommended outing to see this huge rocky amphitheatre between the promontory of Glandasse and S Vercors. Easily reached from Châtillon by D120 to Menée hamlet, then L up the narrow rural farm road D224 to roadhead and old semi-abandoned hamlet of Archiane. Attractive, quaint location (784m), hut with simple accommodation and meals served, trout hatcheries, fine picnic meadow, nearby caves of Tournières. Traces of cultivation, but mostly garrigue-style vegetation with lavender and wild carnation. A great site for photography, especially in autumn when the afternoon light plays on the cliff architecture of the Archiane horseshoe, such as the Tête du Jardin. Notable location for rock climbers and a favourite approach for backpackers heading for the Vercors plateau via GR93.

Col de Menée

1457m S side. Returning to Menée hamlet (636m), one can drive up to the eponymous col along the narrow, steep-sided valley. Admire the well-tailored boxwood hedges along the road. Halfway up is Les Nonnières hamlet and a pleasant luncheon halt at the Auberge du Mont Barral; swimming pool. Go on towards the pass, leaving D515 on L that serves Bénevise hamlet and the Vallée de Combeau track. The road traverses dry, S-facing slopes, then enters pine forest with enticing views upwards to fine green meadows below Crête de Jabouil, overlooked by Mont Barral (1903m), a handsome, roundheaded summit. After Ravin de Combe Noire the road emerges from forest to cross pastures used for skiing in winter at 'stade de neige'. Then the road enters a tunnel 500m ahead under actual col. See the Trièves section of the guide for excursions hereabouts.

– o –

Valdrôme 815m Sources of the river Drôme lie in a remote horse-shoe of upland meadows and forested hills well off the beaten track. This backwater can be reached by a once-a-day minibus from Die but essentially a car is needed. 31km along the N93 from Die, a turning to follow the D306 reaches the village in another 7km. In the final section the traveller is rewarded with vistas of exten-sively wooded slopes and the infant Drôme a flashing torrent in its bed. Formerly a much-inhabited corner of rural France, and a fair-sized village in the old days, Valdrôme seems to have sub-sided into deep sleep. Modern tourism is now making a brave attempt to rouse it from lethargy – with some success.

This is a handsome village built on a prominent spur with many existing houses dating back to the 15th century. Some have been recently refurbished by absentee second-home owners, most of them from the Grenoble or Marseille areas. Of the original inhabitants, a few elderly folk are still in residence. Nowadays, despite billboard adverts along the approach roads proclaiming Station de Valdrôme, the place seems to be developing into a low-profile resort for discerning vacationers in search of peace and quiet away from crowds. Activities alternate between downhill and cross-country skiing, plus excursions on snow shoes in winter. From April to September mountain biking trips are made on the slopes and forest of the resort with group leaders, the ski lifts being used to hoist bikers to the top of La Pyramide. Also in summer there is organised archery, backpacking, rock climbing and trout fishing. In the autumn Valdrôme is almost taken over by hunters – formidable-looking individuals in khaki gaiters, camouflage jackets and jungle caps – who comb surroun-ding hillsides in search of chamois, red deer, roebuck and wild boar.

For information in winter apply to the Valdrôme ski-resort bar/restaurant (75.21.47.24); in summer, to Club Omni-Sport du Haut-Diois, Valdrôme (75.21.40.06). Accommodation available at local gîte d'étape (10 beds only and often fully booked, so phone in advance 75.21.48.32), and Hotel-Restaurant l'Oustaou, a charming little place with friendly proprietress, wholesome cuisine at reasonable prices and capacity for 26 - half of it in a dormitory. In summer there is a camping ground, while furnished rooms may also be rented.

Col du Charron   1319m

Pleasant mid-afternoon stroll to spy out lie of the land. Initially by car ESE from Valdrôme along the D106 Serres road; turn off R past Les Pauvrets towards Le Cheylard, finally parking some 50m from end of metalled road, just short of a farm. Turn L after farm (2 dogs) - ignoring track that heads R down towards another farm some 250m away - and follow yellow flashes for Tour du Duffre. Rather steep stony track recently used by 4WD vehicles and horses. Sparse woodland of oak, boxwood, genet and pine. Last named have suffered through forest fires, but re-afforestation has since occurred with pine saplings and some larch. Slope relents over last section before Col (1h30 from roadhead).

Views over entire N side of Montagne de l'Aup. On ridge itself the track develops into a cross-country skiing circuit. To continue the Tour du Duffre (as the Montagne de l'Aup loop circuit is called) walk about 40m S, then L, where a small wooden signpost indicates direction of La Piarre. Return to roadhead takes about 40 min.

LE DUFFRE   1757m

Long, crescent-shaped ridge with pastures on the N slopes that account for the name Montagne de l'Aup, of which Le Duffre is the culminating point; it presents fairly steep escarpments on the S side. Disappointingly unremarkable when seen from a distance, but its sub-peak, La Pyramide (1734m), marred by skiing development, is somewhat more inviting. Accessible to the average rambler, merely necessitating a short sharp plod up grass slopes. Best time, June and autumn.

Above (S) of Valdrôme, a good road with hairpins and guardrails in the right places attains in 20 min the Valdrôme ski resort. It is so quiet up here, out of season, that a feasibility study for the re-introduction of the brown bear chose Valdrôme forest as the likeliest spot, in mixed coniferous and deciduous trees. Spacious parking-lot in resort (at place marked on maps, Serre de Prorets). Opened in 1983, facilities for ski-hire (downhill) and beginners' classes for cross-country; has large communal building pleasantly situated in grassy hollow opposite nursery slopes. Large bar/restaurant; wooden picnic benches and tables outside beneath pine trees.

Follow R-hand skitow up through pine and fir, with beech showing higher up (Bois du Milieu). Slopes are rather steep but thankfully of grass. Emerge from the forest with views R(WSW) beyond a shepherds' hut to prominent rock outcrops and the fir forest of Montagne de la Sarcéna. Work L(ESE) past departure of La Pyramide skilift and tackle steep grassy slopes slantwise, aiming at the rim of Montagne de l'Aup; most pleasant walking in late spring over flower carpet. As slopes steepen, gradually veer R again till top of skilift is attained and with it, La Pyramide. Duffre now lies SW, beyond a grassy saddle. Descend steep slopes to saddle, then short work on the terminal slopes where some simple rocks and scree make an appearance; small cairn on top. View S to Ventoux, N to Glandasse and Grand Veymont, NE to major peaks of Dévoluy. Presence of yellow flashes along rim, over La Pyramide and up to and beyond summit of Duffre suggest existence of some kind of complete ridge traverse of Montagne de l'Aup (1h30 from carpark to Duffre summit; round trip about 2h15).

Access to this mountain is also possible from Serres via D27 to La Piarre, then W up winding road past Le Vissac to terminus below Col d'Arron (1445m), whence Duffre summit is attainable by steep wooded SE slopes.

– o –

Lus la Croix-Haute 1030m The eastern marches of Drôme consist of a wedge of territory abutting Dévoluy; also separating Trièves from Bochaine proper. Republican France imposed limits on its departments with scant regard for the old regional boundaries. Administratively then, the Lus enclave, or Haut-Bochaine, depends on Die to which it is linked by the N539 via the Gas gorge and Col de Grimone (1318m), itself an interesting jump-off point for various excursions. From the main N-S axis of the N75 trunk road, access is by side roads of one km (bus service).

Within its horseshoe of hills, Lus and a few satellite villages constitute a self-contained unit of field, forest and alpine meadow for dairy farming. The proximity of a cluster of fair-sized peaks – the Lus Aiguilles (Tête de Vachères, 2402m) – attract plentiful precipitation in a NW oriented location conducive to good snow retention on comparatively avalanche-free slopes. No wonder the area has become popular with cross-country buffs, downhill skiers and ski tourers. Since 1983 an annual ski-mountaineering contest, the Grande Trace, attracts to Lus an increasing number of participants. **La Jarjatte** (1150m), the last hamlet in the valley, has become a popular resort for family skiing with its 4 skitows and gentle forest runs (phone 92.58.51.86/92.58.53.66). As the hub of several GR paths, the district has remarkable possibilities for mountain walking; for this reason a Bureau des Guides has been set up (92.58.55.00).

Various kinds of accommodation are available. There are 2 gîtes: Valgabondage (92.58.57.79) at La Jarjatte (no self-catering and meals are provided); Point Virgule at Lus (92.58.57.79), with a capacity of 20 and 17 respectively. Also Les Pervenches at Lus (92.58.50.32), Le Chamousset (92.58.51.12) and 3 other hotel/restaurants with full pension service and moderate prices. For other particulars apply to local Syndicat d'Initiative where VTT may also be hired (92.58.51.85). Pony trekking is popular and Les Pervenches is a centre for this activity.

JOCOU 2051m

Montagne de Jocou, a flattened pyramid and famed viewpoint, is the highest part of a N-S ridge presenting a lumpish outline when seen from Trièves. The deep cleft of Col de Seysse, and steep N slopes of Crête de l'Archat (2007m) in particular, attract the eye in winter, being extensively snow covered. This partly explains the presence at the outlet of the main E-facing cwm of the ailing Lalley-le-Jocou ski facility. The mountain is also and mainly a strategic bridge between Vercors and Bochaine, with backpackers following the GR93 footpath over its summit in summer.

Direct E side. Short, brutal, tough route; pathless. Coming along the N75 from N, turn off a few m N of inn (bus stop) at Col de la Croix-Haute (1176m, not clearly signposted). Potholed road W zigzags up to Lalley-le-Jocou (1355m). Large parking area and one or two communal buildings; in 1992 it looked rather rundown with junk (smashed fences and discarded skitow equipment) and large flocks of sheep milling round.

From carpark head up grassy slopes gradually trending S; keep to L (E) of Les Adorais skitow and aim towards Col du Salut. On approaching col avoid tendency to trend R up steepening slopes; go along line of skitow to its terminus, cross fence running W, then go R (W) up reasonable grass slope, keeping fence on your R. The slope soon steepens into rough stony terrain and tussocks. Climb this tediously in short zags about 50m distance from fence to finish on a flat grassy terrace below scree slopes and long rock band. Traverse L(S) along grass and climb to L end of rockband.

Go up a little gully with small tree at top on skyline edge. Ascend this edge along top of rockband, steep comfortable rocks, to an obvious large flat spot at top of highest point of rockband below and at foot of Jocou ESE upper spur (c1800m). Now with summit in view ascend 2 broad steps tediously along line of spur over easy flagstone rocks, rubble and grass, to finish up summit pyramid. About 2h30 and 1h30 in descent.

The normal route on S side of mountain, though longer and with a bigger vertical interval, is altogether more relaxing. Above **Grimone** hamlet (2 gîtes, often booked up), from the D539 Col de Grimone road at pt.1293, 2 waymarked access paths from road lead N over scrub into the Jocou forest, and onward in zigzags under the sharp Amousières ridge to turn its headland (1943m) R and reach the main ridge at a fine grassy saddle. Go along crest in a splendid position to top (3h-3h15 from road).

COL DES AIGUILLES 2005m

Classic excursion from La Jarjatte (1150m), accessible to walkers in dry conditions, May-October. Also popular with ski-tourers, mid-January to early April; feasible after first snows in suitable footwear and with ski-pole. From tiny 'main' square in Lus, turn sharp L(N), then first R(SE) along rough metalled road (under improvement) beside camp ground and drive for 5km to La Jarjatte. Turn R into hamlet and park vehicles (not much room) near main resort building at end of metalled road. The next turning R(SW) leads in 100m to the popular Valgabondage gîte (see Lus, above). Taxi service from Lus to La Jarjatte.

Go along unmade forest road SE for one km, then take a track E to cross La Jarjatte ski-area and work up Ravin des Aiguilles towards the col. So reach end of broad track opposite a skilift. Now follow on L waymarked GR94, signposted Col des Aiguilles, with red/white flashes through mixed forest of fir, boxwood and oak, and a stony torrent for company on R. After some 15 min an intersection with GR94C (heading off R to St-Julien-en-Bochaîne) is encountered. Turn L as you reach maintenance track - all nicely signposted - then turn off R again, still heading E with the stony streambed on R. After some 10 min another skitow is passed (nice rearward views towards Toussière, qv). In another 10 min reach another maintenance track serving the top station of ski installations. Go on without difficulty, relying on red/white marks and emerge above tree line at the foot of scree slopes running up to the col (1h45).

On the L(N) rises a line of very dry, sheer Dolomite-like cliffs leading to the culminating Tête de Vachères (2402m). Keep on up steepening slopes to foot of terminal couloir between Serre Long and Mt Bouffet. Work up zigzags to col (cairn), fine view E down Vallon des Aiguilles. Climb L for about 50m for optimum view of Pic de Bure and Super-Dévoluy ski resort slopes (1h15, 3h from La Jarjatte). Descend the same way.

The impressive rock peaks either side of the col are mostly (but not entirely) seriously loose for climbers; all have been ascended by a variety of routes.

– o –

Some mountains in adjoining districts can be ascended from the Lus centre, and these are so identified later in the guide.

Lus-la-Croix-Haute village at entrance to upper Buëch (Jarjatte) valley.

89

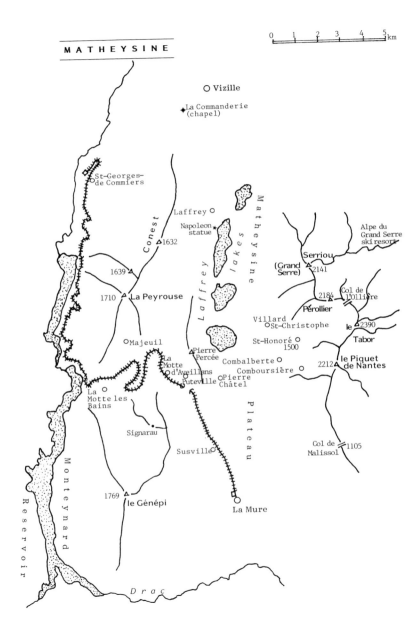

MATHEYSINE

0 1 2 3 4 5 km

○ Vizille

✦ La Commanderie
(chapel)

◇ St-Georges-
de Commiers

○ Laffrey

Conest

△1632

★ Napoleon
statue

Laffrey lakes

Matheysine

Alpe du
Grand Serre
ski resort

Serriou

△ 1639

(Grand
Serre)
△2141

1710 △ La Peyrouse

△2184 Col de
l'Ollière

Pérollier

○ Majeuil

Villard
○ St-Christophe

le △2390

Tabor

St-Honoré ○
1500

La
Motte
○ d'Aveillans
Puteville

Pierre
Percée

Combalberte ○

Comboursière ○

le Piquet
△2212 de Nantes

La ○
Motte les
Bains

Pierre
○ Châtel

Plateau

• Signarau

Susville ○

Col de
Malissol 1105

1769 △
le Génépi

○
La Mure

Monteynard

Reservoir

Drac

MATHEYSINE LAKES REGION

Looking SE from Grenoble the observer cannot fail to notice the asymmetrical cone of Grand Serre and the twin humps of Conex and Génépi, especially when their snowy outlines stand out against the deep blue sky of a crisp January morning. Between them, hollowed out by Ice Age glaciers, lies the windswept, lake-studded upland plateau of Matheysine (derived from Maltasaina, original Latin form, Mattacenus).

This is one of the coldest inhabited areas of Isère and it has nurtured a rare specimen - the basic Dauphinois stock, or Matheysin, as he is called. A dour, practical, short-spoken individual, once initial reserve has thawed he may well become a friend, tried and true. The butt of numerous jokes and unflattering anecdotes, here is one of many obtained first hand from a genuine Matheysin:

> *Consider one hundred Matheysins;*
> *Ninety-nine of them are rascals.*
> *What of the only honest one?*
> *He's in prison; what for?*
> *He found and took home a piece of rope*
> *Which had a cow tied to the other end!*

Matheysins have experienced a long and intimate intercourse with the land in a struggle for survival. Pasturing their sheep and goats on Génépi and Serriou (as Grand Serre was known when it belonged to Margaret of Burgundy); eking out a wretched existence from lakeside fields; trampled underfoot by medieval lords; periodically plundered by the dregs of Europe's warring armies. The opening of coal mines near La Mure (mura = an allusion to the town's former walls) at the end of the 19th century came as a long hoped-for blessing. Nowadays, with a waning coal industry, the grimy little town, sitting on the edge of the plateau with the Drac at its feet and the hulking mass of Obiou to the S, has had to adapt to the times. Of late it has undergone a thorough clean-up, with an attractive shopping precinct and numerous flowers gracing the High Street near the recently refurbished townhall.

Tourism has become a major source of revenue, centred on the Route Napoleon and the Napoleonic legend. You are not allowed to forget this. Apart from the great man's equestrian statue, the locals will even point to a piece of woodland, above Lake Laffrey at the foot of Grand Serre, with an outline supposedly resembling an Imperial eagle.

The Laffrey lakes provide fishing, swimming and sailboarding, backed up by good local gastronomy (try *gratin dauphinois*) and a few hotels, gîtes and B & B places which function chiefly in summer. Two ski developments have been somewhat lacklustre and these sites are noted in descriptions. Grenoble also exercises a honeypot effect on the area; many local residents commute to work in the city. Others do so from nearby La Motte d'Aveillans, a beautifully sited, exceptionally healthy hillside location barely 30 min drive from Grenoble.

La Mure scenic railway

One of the main tourist attractions of the Dauphiné, and a historic oddity in its own right. A daring piece of engineering undertaken over a century ago - 18 tunnels hacked out of the rock, 6 crazily suspended viaducts, and 32km of narrow gauge track from Saint Georges-de-Commiers (315m) to La Mure (881m) - such is this picturesque little railway opened in 1888 to haul coal from the local mines. Now that installations in Susville are only producing a little anthracite for industrial needs, the railway survives as a well-publicised means of introducing visitors to a neglected corner of Dauphiné. Ideal for Senior Citizens; indeed, on most trains running in season, at least 3 coaches out of 6 are reserved for them.

Trains normally run from early April to mid October. In summer it is advisable to avoid Sundays, and always arrive well before departure time. Cars may be parked beneath a large cedar outside St-Georges station - which may also be reached from Grenoble by the morning SNCF railcar serving Veynes. A quaint little electric locomotive of the 1930s hauls antiquated wooden carriages of similar vintage which, for all their age, are well maintained.

Once underway, the train clatters up through tunnel and cutting, carriages creaking and swaying, taking one back to the dawn of rail travel. The line is hemmed in by undergrowth along the early stages; as height is gained there are evolving vistas of forested gorge and cliffs of the Vercors rising into view in the distance. Between 2 tunnels one peeps down at the Monteynard reservoir, much beloved by sailboarders and waterskiers, but also visited in comfort and decorum by La Mira Miniature Cruises (76.34.14.56). Maintaining a dignified pace the train swings E to reach La-Motte-les-Bains, passing the down train in the process, with glimpses of a castle surrounded by a canopy of green, now a rehabilitation centre for drug addicts. Then the line makes a prolonged detour along the N flank of Génépi, before cautiously negotiating the breath-taking Loulla viaducts, and edging back towards La Motte d'Aveillans, with Conest (1710m) in full view ahead. At La Motte a 15 min halt enables honey and wine merchants to ply their trade with captive travellers. Off again, the train dives into the Festinière tunnel – at 925m the highest point on the line – for the final stretch past semi-derelict mine installations of Susville, and some drab if tidy little houses, to the terminus at La Mure with the Obiou (2789m) dominating the background.

After being jolted around for a couple of hours, passengers are delighted to walk into the town centre – only minutes away – where a variety of restaurants await patronage. Recommended is Mathey's inn, excellent cuisine, cheerful proprietor and reasonable prices (76.81.24.65); also La Rose des Sables, La Bergerie and several small café/restaurants.

TABOR 2389m

The highest peak of the Matheysine lakes region, this Mont Tabor (also Thabor), not to be confused with its bigger Briançonnais cousin, would appear to owe its name to a vague resemblance with its Biblical namesake, or so it seemed to pilgrims homeward bound from Palestine as they crossed La Mure plateau. In reality it is a fairly prominent knoll emerging from an otherwise mundane ridge running N-S for some 10km from the unexciting Grand Serre (2141m), defiled by skitows, to the Malissol pass. Something of a grind in summer, it becomes a stimulating undertaking in the period November-March, with scope for ice axe and crampons, or seal skins and knives in the ski touring mode, on the upper stretches of the mountain. The following description is based on an ascent made in near winter conditions during a particularly snow-free time in February 1993.

From St-Honoré-1500 ski resort. Signposted everywhere on the Matheysine plateau and clearly visible from afar, chiefly due to a pair of hideous yellow cranes idle since 1991. Road twists and turns past Fugière and Combalberte, the latter boasting a Gîte de France. Leaving Comboursière to the R, drive up to ski resort. In early 1993 this presented all the rubble and rubbish of an unfinished building site, 3 blocks of flats being completed, and more to come if and when the project resumes, with several 'For Sale' signs. Leave vehicles at end of parking area near start of the Domaine de la Chaud chairlift.

General line of attack is almost due E up steep slopes opposite car park, climbing direct to skyline. Take path heading E across a clearing, then L(NE) into conifers up a broad track. Turn R at small building (pumping station?), to veer L again later, following at first red, eventually yellow, marks on rocks. Track now bears off into Ollière cwm between Pérollier and Tabor. Leave it and turn R at intersection where waymarks indicate Tabor to L and Piquet de Nantes to R. Track now makes several long zigzags, at first through conifers, then across open, steep avalanche-prone mountainside. Because of avalanche hazard, extensive plantation of conifers extends halfway up main slope, while a cable line rather resembling a skitow, but equipped to transport explosive charges destined to trigger avalanches, runs overhead to a high rocky point overlooking Ollière cwm. Track eventually peters out; continue to follow yellow flashes, alternating between path and a succession of horizontal platforms, 2-3m wide, also designed with avalanche protection in mind.

After the last platform, path veers ESE (intermittent yellow marks) and ascends across moderately steep scree and dwarf juniper in direction of Piquet de Nantes. Near lip of cwm that now appears to R, turn L (due E) and make straight up final slopes (rocks and snow) to broad rounded ridge, known as Crête des Barres (2250m, approx. 2h15 from start).

Summit of Tabor now looms to L(NNE), standing slightly proud of the main ridge and appearing somewhat steep due to foreshortening. Follow ridge with sheer drops to the Roizonne valley on R(E). Once a shallow saddle is reached, head E up a moderate slope; turn an outcrop on its L(N) side and so embark on a gentle incline that soon levels out at the top (1h30 from Crête des Barres; 3h45 from St-Honoré-1500). Fine view E over deep trench of Roizonne valley to very alpine looking peak of Grand Armet (2792m); a small glacier nestles in its N cwm; also NE to Taillefer and Chamrousse. Views S extend over the whole of Dévoluy and to hills beyond Gap.

Normal itinerary for ski tourers and for descent on foot. Follow ridge N from Tabor to col adjoining Oreille du Loup. Then turn L and head W down a series of gullies, vague traces and quite steep in places, gradually working NW as the Ollière col and chairlift beneath it come into sight.

Failsafe route is to steer past Achard tarn to reach a broad track, whence, on turning L, St-Honoré-1500 may be reached after a long walk through coniferous forest. To avoid numerous bothersome zigzags and ups and downs, it is preferable to strike W before Charlet tarn and come out on traversing path, bearing L (yellow flashes), that returns more rapidly back to ski resort (2h15 down from Tabor summit. For round trip, allow at least 6h).

LA PEYROUSE 1710m

This softly rounded top is the culminating point of the long ridge variously marked Montagne de Conest, or Conex (in 18th century, Montagne de Vaux); the second highest elevation among the hills lying W of the Matheysine plateau. Well forested on the W flank, more sparsely wooded on the E, it consists mostly of excellent upland pasture above the 1500m contour. Approachable from several directions, the following applies to the most rewarding way by the S ridge from Majeuil. A very safe mountain from late spring onwards. Community bus from La Mure goes through La Motte d'Aveillans (D529) near SE foot of mountain. Bus stop at Le Mollard, 1.5km from Majeuil hamlet roadhead (960m). Park a car near former holiday camp building. Recommended.

Follow path that heads W along wire fence, with fields to the R, into Majeuil Combe and cross stream that comes meandering down through woods. At a fork ignore path that heads R up the stream; likewise a path heading L, apparently back to hamlet. Instead, take fairly obvious trod making an ascending traverse of open, grassy slopes in general SW direction. After crossing narrow gully (spring), path climbs through pine and juniper to reach pt. 1161 on S ridge of mountain (30 min). Go N up broad forested ridge with bald summit in full view. The subsequent ascent through pine forest, with clearings alternating with thickly wooded patches (wrens scolding from thickets, or buzzards mewing in the middle distance) is a delightful experience. Some of the pines are gnarled and weather beaten; many of the juniper bushes present a handsome, tapering cypress-like silhouette; an occasional fir is seen, out of place on this southerly exposure.

Although the path is totally unmarked, route finding is no problem. The obvious trod heads unerringly onwards, eventually up the ridge with some quite steep sections. The terminal slopes (with residual snow patches in spring) are occasionally glimpsed through the branches. Emerge above the tree-line onto steep pasture. Now work R, crossing several cow trails, to reach a raised part of the ridge, with slightly stonier, rockier ground underfoot which is followed to the summit. The top plays host to scientific data-collecting devices comprising a small, locked wooden shack on stilts (looks like a garden lavatory); a 15m mast supporting 2 solar panels and a mysterious steel rod; no inscription whatsoever (2h30 from Majeuil).

Interesting view NNE along flattish ridge to nearby pt. 1639 overlooking a little tarn, with another one (Petit Lac) visible further away at foot of Conex pt. 1632. Conspicuous tracks suggest that farmers use 4WD vehicles up here in summer to milk their cows. Fine views E are to be had of Grand Serre, Pérollier and Tabor, with Grand Armet in far background. Return the same way.

A   B

GÉNÉPI 1769m

Also Sénépy, Séneppi, possibly another example of IGN high-handed change of spelling of a regional name (cf. Ménis/Ménil et al). A Y-shaped, smooth-sloped mountain of lush cow pasture and thick forest; the highest Matheysine summit W of the Laffrey lakes. Various approaches: directly from La Mure, and a favourite with local town dwellers; along S ridge from Mayres-Savel; up forested W slopes from Les Arnauds; or the author's route from near La Motte d'Aveillans – a pleasant stroll revealing fine views of Trièves and Dévoluy. Recommended.

From La Motte d'Aveillans on the D529 (see La Peyrouse, above), side road D115d at the place called La Festinière (964m) is followed W and S uphill for 3km to **Signarau** (1239m) ski facility, communal building (for cross-country skiers) and gîte d'étape. 400m ahead parking space at foot of steep grassy slopes adorned by skitow (1280m). From here a twisting and confusing 4WD track mounts eastwards; ignore this.

Due S, follow skitow straight up to rounded shoulder and grassy saddle close to tree line. By means of various footpaths, work steadily L(SE), aiming for the flattish ridge of the Côte de l'Aup. This gives plain walking due S, passing under a power line, and at one point along 4WD track, then bearing SW along narrow trace past pt. 1617, from where a descent is made to the Col de Sénépy (1526m). Much trampled muddy site with cattle hut and watering troughs for animals. Head directly SW up steep slopes to reach a broad track that winds up to summit pasture; small concrete shelter, cattle enclosure and rain water pool (1h30 from Signarau).

Fascinating prospects of the Grand Veymont, Mont Aiguille and Obiou. Coming down, go back to the muddy col, then follow a distinct trod along W side of the Côte de l'Aup. One or two outcrops and stone-slides are negotiated until the going becomes simpler along one of the many drailles that mark contour lines across the slopes. Further N reach a lower section of the 4WD track going down to the road within a short distance of the skitow (about 1h).

PIERRE PERCÉE 1240m

Formerly Pierre-Pertuisade, or Pierra Partizia, one of the Seven Wonders of Dauphiné, this strange arched rock stands near the top of Creys hill overlooking the SW side of Pierre-Châtel lake. According to legend, it represents the devil at prayer after being turned to stone as a result of his defeat by Lesdiguières, the great protestant military leader of the late 16th century.

Access from Pierre-Châtel village (926m), or La Festinière (see

Génépi, above), bus services. From latter take small road NE marked: Putteville, la Pierre Percée. After Putteville hamlet and a couple of bends, cars can be parked on space provided near the Pierre Percée signpost at entrance to broad country lane. Follow lane up a large curve and bear L at a bend halfway uphill, along a narrow track. This makes a short detour W before heading due N over pastures to the rock which has been visible throughout the approach. Impatient souls should resist temptation to shortcut across fields by crawling under barbed wire and clambering over hedges – definitely frowned upon by local farmers. From the top, instructive view S over Étang du Crey, the Susville mining installations, La Mure, and to the Obiou. Much frequented on Sundays by walkers and mountain bikers (30 min from carpark).

La Mure narrow gauge scenic railway.

Top: Pierre-Châtel village, looking E to Picquet de Nantes-Tabor ridge across the ☐theysine plateau. Pérollier, far L.

☐ttom: L to R: Rocher Rond, Tête de Vallon Pierra, Grand Ferrand, E side seen from ☐ar Agnières-en-Dévoluy.

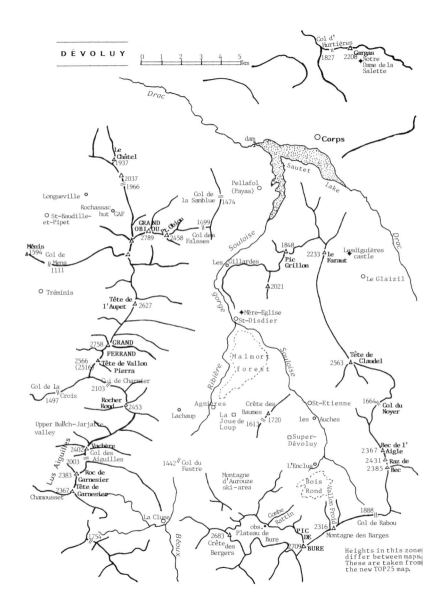

DÉVOLUY

0 1 2 3 4 5 km

Col d' Hurtières 1827

Gargas 2208
Notre Dame de la Salette

Drac

dam

Corps

Sautet lake

Drac

Le Châtel 1937

2037
1966

Longueville

Rochassac hut CAF

St-Baudille-et-Pipet

Col de la Samblue 1474

Pellafol (Payas)

GRAND OBIOU Pt Obiou 2789 2458

1699
Col des Falsses

Ménis 1594
Col de Mens 1111

Les Gillardes

Souloise

Pic Grillon 1848

2233 le Faraut

Lesdiguières castle

Le Glaizil

2021

Tréminis

Tête de l'Aupet 2627

Ribière gorge

Mère-Eglise
St-Disdier

Souloise

2758 GRAND FERRAND

2566 (2516) Tête de Vallon Pierra

Col de la Croix 1497

Col de Charnier 2103

Rocher Rond 2453

Malmort forest

Tête de Claudel 2563

Col du Noyer 1664

Upper Buëch-Jarjatte valley

Agnières

Lachaup

Crête des Baumes

La Joue de Loup 1613 1720

St-Etienne

les Auches

Lus Aiguilles

2402 Vachère
Col des Aiguilles 2003

Roc de Garnesier 2383
Tête de Garnesier 2367

Chamousset

1754

1442 Col du Festre

Montagne d'Aurouze ski-area

Super-Dévoluy

L'Enclus

Bois Rond

Béoux

La Cluse

2683 Plateau de Bure
Crête des Bergers

obs.

Combe Ratin

PIC DE BURE
2709

2316
2367

Bec de l' Aigle 2367
2431 Raz de 2385 Bec

Vallon Froid

1888
Col de Rabou
Montagne des Barges

Heights in this zone differ between maps. These are taken from the new TOP25 map.

DÉVOLUY

The name emanates either from Dévolus or Dévolutus = handing down of rights (as in a feudal land deed); or, more likely, from the verb *devolere* = to roll, an allusion to extensive scree and boulderfields that characterize the area.

The loftiest and most rugged of all Prealpine massifs, Dévoluy is even more of a natural citadel than Vercors, representing a unique tract of high, remote country shut off from the world and featuring 2 starkly beautiful outlying promontories - Obiou and Pic de Bure - that stand out proudly from surrounding lowlands. An almost perfect basin of syncline, walled in by uncompromising precipice and hanging screefields. The only easy access is from the N via the spectacular Souloise gorge and its swift-flowing trout stream, or from S through the Potrachon defile (permanently threatened by landslides) and over the Col du Festre. Apart from the Col du Noyer (1664m) that provides motorized access from the Gap-Corps road during the summer months, all other ways involve foot-slogging over mountain passes such as Col de Charnier, Col de Rabou and Col des Aiguilles.

In this weird, secluded, time-forgotten world of deep limestone chasms - known here as *choroun,* and mammoth scree slopes known as *clapiers,* till the early Middle Ages Dévoluy was mainly the summer residence of transhumants who used to leave it in winter to the custody of eagles and wolves, its original denizens. Permanent human habitation came in the 11th century with the arrival of monks. At that time Cluse was founded, and the Mère-Eglise at Gicon, near St-Disdier, one of the oldest and best preserved specimens of Romance architecture, seems also to have been built. Throughout the feudal era the area developed slowly with its pastoral and small holding farm communities. At the start of the present century, Dévoluy was saddled with an unenviable reputation as an accursed mountain because of its hellish scree, the 'Siberia of Hautes-Alpes', and the abode of smelly shepherds accused of having wantonly devastated local woodlands. This charge was less than fair as forests had never been particularly widespread in the area. At the present time, only 7% of the terrain is wooded. All the same, A W Andrews*, who visited in 1905, scathingly dismissed Dévoluy

* Notable English rock climber and alpinist (1868-1959), best remembered as the inventor of climbing on the Cornwall granite cliffs in 1902; also reached semi-finals of the Mens Tennis singles at Wimbledon in 1900.

as being merely "the stones of emptiness, as barren as part of Sinai described in the Old Testament...deep crevices and cracks many yards wide which went down to unknown depths".

Like other mountain fastnesses Dévoluy has paid its toll in rural exodus. From 2063 inhabitants in 1846, the population had dwindled to 885 in 1975, with a density nowhere higher than 4.75 inhab./sq.km. Human beings are heavily outnumbered by sheep – a cross bred strain of Merino adapted to local conditions; some 27,000 were to be found in the region in 1980. By contrast, less than 300 head of cattle are raised in the entire massif. Sheep-rearing remains essentially geared to regional market requirements, focussing on breeding 4-5 month-old lambs that buyers from Sisteron and Veynes come up to collect on the spot.

But if Dévoluy has become better known to the outside world, this is chiefly attributable to winter sports. Places like Agnières get about 1200mm annual rainfall with, as a corollary, extensive snow cover on N-facing slopes. Promoters from Marseille in the mid 1960s were quick to see the possibilities of the Montagne d'Aurouze (an attractive combination of gentle slopes, ample snow and plentiful sunshine). The Société des Grands Travaux de Marseille started work in 1966-67 on the so-called 'intergrated resort' of Super-Dévoluy – the first of its kind in the Alps. Centred on a single gigantic apartment block – soon dubbed by locals *le paquebot des neiges* (liner of the snows) – this controversial all-in-one, self contained unit with its 6000+ beds, functioning well apart from traditional village life and services has, in the final analysis, led to remarkably little friction between local people and holiday skiers. Moreover, the N537/D17 road that serves 'Super-Dév' from Veynes has been beautifully surfaced to give Marseille based visitors a trouble-free drive. A later development, and something of an improvement on the Super-Dévoluy eye-sore, the satellite resort of Joue-du-Loup presents a low profile with its relatively small and congenial sloping-roofed buildings offering some 2700 beds. The combined skiing area extends from 1470 to 2510m and comprises 4 skitows and 27 chairlifts. The locality also caters for cross-country skiers, and features a shopping arcade, skating rink and swimming pool. Information: 92.58.82.80. Regular bus services. In summer the usual multi-activity package: horse riding, backpacking, tennis, rock climbing and pot-holing.

Parallel with ski development, mountaineers have not been idle in the massif. Apart from René Desmaison's exploits on Pic de Bure and an annual ski-mountaineering contest of exceptionally high standard, the more staid variety of mountain tourer has also contributed to making of Dévoluy one of the more sought-after areas

102

2682

Crête des Bergers from the Potrachon defile (SW), Dévoluy.

of the Alps. The various GR93/94 Tour de l'Obiou and/or Tour du Dévoluy combinations have become favourites with backpackers. However, they are excursions for the tried and tested hiker with a head for heights (some footpaths are quite exposed). Proper footwear and familiarity with steep rough ground are prerequisites. Water is scarce and should always be carried. Notwithstanding these remarks, Dévoluy must surely rank as the premier area for mountain walking described in this guidebook.

Rock climbing

Many quite important odds and ends apart (mostly on the Obiou), there are 2 famous Dévoluy climbs: the classic E Pillar Desmaison route (1961) on Pic de Bure, with a 2h+ approach from Enclus via Brèche de Bure to foot of wall, yielding 500m of TD+ in 8-10h, and descent recommended by Combe Rattin. Much less frequented, the Crête des Bergers (2682m) at W end of Bure plateau, by its Charbonnier/Lainez route giving 450m of TD climbing; accessible from Cluse in 2-3h to base of cliff; descent by Combe d'Agnières. This was the scene of the greatly lamented fatal accident from stonefall to the noted alpinist Jean Couzy in 1958. In more recent times a number of 450-500m routes have been pioneered on the perfectly accessible Gillardes cliffs (45 min from road) extending for one km along E side of the Souloise gorge below St-Disdier. For further information on serious climbing in Dévoluy, contact François Chaix at the Bureau des guides Dévoluy-Buëch at La Roche des Arnauds (92.57.87.40).

Accommodation

Gîtes d'étape at St-Disdier (Gîte du Renard) and Agnières, also a riverside camping ground between the two, at La Combe de l'Eau. Further gîtes are situated at Col du Festre and St-Etienne; the latter has a bunkhouse, a fully equipped self-catering kitchen and bath-house; also large campsite adjoining, all grouped under the name Les Auches. St-Disdier has a little hotel-restaurant: Neyrette. Further information and accommodation at La Joue du Loup (92.58.83.57) and Super-Dévoluy (92.58.82.80) resorts.

GRANDE TÊTE DE L'OBIOU 2789m

Or simply, Obiou, apparently derived from Testo do biou = Tête de Boeuf in local patois (a common alpine name), monarch of the area and the highest peak described in this guide. Old legends claim that Obiou is a petrified former giant that finally vanquished its rivals Pic de Bure and Grand Ferrand after a lengthy rock-hurling match - as good an explanation as any for the ubiquitous rubble that adorns Dévoluy slopes. Claims that the Mediterranean is visible from the summit are quite fanciful and groundless. By 1876 the peak had been regularly frequented; in that year the CAF fixed a cable (now gone) on La Cravatte section. By then a certain Bourcelot, one of several local hunters available as guides, had already climbed the mountain 4 times. Then came a couple of British 'firsts': Thornton Marshall with 2 guides, 12 August 1879; W A B Coolidge with Jean Isnard, 31 August 1881. The first recorded winter ascent was by Louis Roger and party, 14 January 1928; skis were used for part of the way. Snow cover seems to have been more extensive in those days; in fact, in 1919 and again in 1960, we find allusions to a small glacier, the Casse-Fouira snow patch (not always visible in recent years) on the N side. This side was the scene, in 1950 and 1957, of 2 spectacularly gruesome air-crashes. The classic NW face zigzag was done by a French party in 1927. It is only grade II+, with lots of walking/scrambling, but also narrow and exposed foot ledges and a series of steep chimneys in the upper section. The E face was first climbed in 1940, and modern routes of grade V/VI on other facets up to 400m high were first achieved in 1970.

This handsome, distinctive mountain at the NW corner of Dévoluy entirely overshadows the scene when travelling along the Route Napoleon between La Mure and Corps. A truly noble summit of alpine proportions, it is much sought-after by peak-baggers and is a regular venue for Grenoble based rock climbers. The ascent is shorter and less of a grind than the slightly lower rival Grand Ferrand. Difficulties that may occur halfway up and higher are calculated to test the mettle of the ordinary mountain walker. Once the rocks and schist ledges are wet, the mountain becomes dangerous and should be avoided by everyone. Under snow it rates as a serious alpine project. Best season, July to October. There are residual snow patches in June, though the slopes were still under snow, for example, in first week of July in 1992. A rope of 20m could come in handy.

Normal route. E and S flanks approached from N. Grade I+. On the latest TOP25 map #3337 0T, the route is clearly indicated in red. From the Route Napoleon N85 on the N outskirts of Corps, turn S and W down the D537, alongside Sautet barrage lake and dam (latter is a popular bungee bridge-jumping site), and go up onto the Pellafol plateau to Les Payas (Pellafol); community bus. A lane SW goes up past a small reservoir to start of a forest road. This is a decent stony track that winds up through firs to Col de la Samblue (1474m); forestry hut and picnic site. Continue up to spacious parking lot on a saddle near the spot marked 'grottes

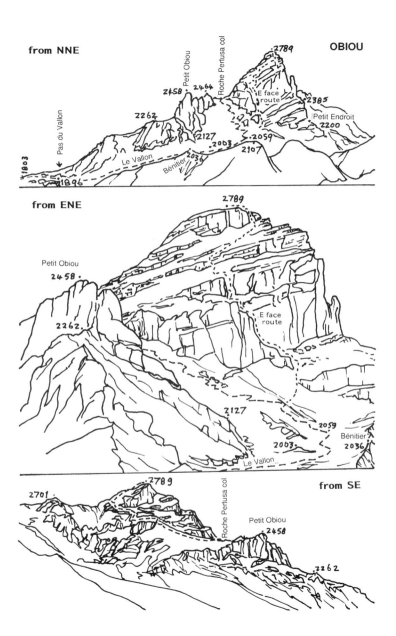

from NNE   **OBIOU**

2789

Petit Obiou

2458   2464

Roche Pertusa col

E face route

2385

Petit Endroit 2200

2262

Pas du Vallon

2127

2059

2003

2107

Le Vallon

Bénitier 2036

1803

1896

from ENE

2789

Petit Obiou

2458

E face route

2262

2127

2059

Bénitier 2036

2003

Le Vallon

from SE

2701

2789

Roche Pertusa col

Petit Obiou

2458

2262

1562m' on TOP25 map.   Placard with usual warning to alpinists to keep dogs on lead, respect environment, etc.   Hunters are very much in evidence in autumn; they must be *persona grata* because the noticeboard doesn't mention them.

Leave carpark via barrier and head straight up track, then path, to Col des Faïsses (1699m); here a sort of shepherd's bothy could be used as a bivouac.   Turn R (due W) and follow well worn path along ridge towards the mountain, now soaring impressively.   As ridge narrows, just past pt.1803, a path arrives from the R; this variant can be used as a shortcut from carpark, snaking up over grass and through stunted pine.

After a short riser, path climbs first rockbands at Pas du Vallon (1896m), an easy but slightly exposed traverse above steep drops. Wine red waymarks are now observed.   Continue by path over gently undulating grass covered terrain, le Vallon, usually with sheep in evidence.   Path now skirts a succession of old moraines and grassy hollows under S flank of Le Bénitier (2036m), then swings S past pt.1998 to confront the Petit Obiou cwm, an enormous débris-filled cirque hemmed in by cliffs; savage view up to Roche Pertusa col between Petit and Grand Obiou (1h15 from carpark).

Zigzags first up grass (Pré Perdu) then scree on R(W) side of cwm lead to start of a long and sometimes exposed ascending traverse L(S).   Vague path crosses outward sloping rock for 50m, then goes up more reassuring rock staircase, with 35-40° scree slopes to the L.   As the rock barrier enclosing screes of the lower part of cwm extends L to merge with rockfaces of Petit Obiou opposite, the rough path becomes a little easier.   Negotiate crumbling masonry mounting to foot of final headwall below col.   This section, initially worrying, is easier than it looks, and consists of none too solid schist occurring in parallel ledges 15-30cm wide, cluttered with débris, and inclined from 30° to 45°.   Waymarks, now appearing more frequently, lead up towards the headwall via a 30m scree and rock staircase, then to the R by several zigzags, returning L for a final *mauvais pas* to circumvent a projecting spur, and a 20m scramble to emerge on path just below the Roche Pertusa col (2470m) (1h30).

Follow path due W up steepening scree, working L to reach foot of arête that enables one to outflank the terminal buttresses - now seen at close quarters.   Scramble up arête by a series of smooth, gently tilted slabs; after 70m the finish is slightly tricky due to undercut holds.   Path then contours L under summit headland, following a series of ledges passing beneath overhangs.   This portion, known as La Cravatte, is easily followed by keeping to numerous paint flashes, with one fairly exposed bit; otherwise the presence of precipices to L is sensed rather than actually obser-ved. The last part is an ascending traverse R, emerging on plain rock slope, scree and thistle, that gradually leads up to the summit cross. An unroofed rock shelter nearby serves as a windbreak. Magnificent summit panorama. On a cloudy day in September, 40 persons were seen on top - some female shivering in ultra short shorts; on a fine weekend day in July-August, 100 or so is not uncommon (1h15, 4h from carpark).

On the descent exercise caution when negotiating the slabs, and below col the first part over schist ledges. Danger of stonefall if several parties are moving down in succession (allow 3h all told).

GRAND FERRAND 2758m

The second summit of Dévoluy; name is variously interpreted as stemming from the Latin *ferus* = wild, or from the French *gris de fer,* with reference to the iron-grey colour of its rocks. A handsome, sharply defined peak; its precipitous 1800m W flank dominates the cirque of Tréminis, from which its impressive proportions are best admired. No record of early ascents; it had apparently been climbed on several occasions before 1844. First British ascent by W A B Coolidge, F Gardiner, 23 September 1888.

Normal route. Grade I. Hazardous in poor visibility and/or rain. At the foot of the long SW spur of the mountain, Col de la Croix (1497m) can be reached in several ways, from the N, W and S. The shortest is given, from the S, from La Jarjatte (gîte); in Diois part of guide, see Lus la Croix-Haute and Col des Aiguilles.

Beyond La Jarjatte the metalled road NE (D505) is followed past campsite and holiday buildings for over 3km to pt.1214, where a track forks L, waymarks and signpost; narrow slot for parking a car. The track soon leads to steep wooded slope where a clear path goes up directly N to Col de la Croix (45 min). On the other side is a longer approach from Tréminis.

Now join GR93 running E and skirting top of forest to N, then zig-zag up grassy slopes to Col des Aurias (1762m), only a shoulder really on the main SW spur. Continue up NE with red/white flashes to make an ascending traverse E along top of steep lower slopes of Tête du Lauzon (sheep may be pasturing here in morning) to reach a broad grassy terrace (2016m) at foot of the Tête's upper scree slopes. Descend slightly, bearing E, leaving improbable weed-choked Lauzon tarn and cliff-edge Source du Lauzon on R. Climb rocky path NE to Col de Charnier (2103m) (1h45 from Col de la Croix).

Grand Ferrand summit area from E.

From here to summit follow conspicuous yellow flashes, sometimes in conjunction with red ones (appearing old and rather worn). First make a horizontal traverse NE, well above the line of GR93, across grassy slopes to circumvent base of the intervening Tête de Vallon Pierra (2516m). On reaching the Clos Rognon the path turns L(NW) and starts climbing into the scree-filled Vallon Froid. Unlikely clumps of stinging-nettles may be encountered – a variety that seems to do equally well on grass and scree. After a well marked ascending scree traverse R, followed by more troublesome scree, emerge on a N-S oriented rib. Go up this to a grassy terrace (yellow flashes).

Now mount sub-vertical scree, following a visible trod to entrance of a chimney; climb this with some moderate scrambling on a rock step halfway up, to exit R near a conspicuous cairn. From here go straight up successive short steep scree terraces – vintage Dévoluy terrain – to gain summit ridge. Go L(W) along this with steep drops on R(N) into upper cwm of Vallon du Grand Villard. A rock step is taken on large holds, after which a vague trace reappears near small shelter beneath an overhang; finish up onto rounded summit screefield (2h45 from Col de Charnier, 4h30 from Col de la Croix, 5h15 from road at pt.1214).

For coming down it is imperative to follow yellow waymarks on first section over sloping scree terraces, down to cairn indicating top of rockband step and chimney feature.

Not yet explored by the author's parties, an approach from the SE side, starting at Lachaup hamlet, gîte (1392m) is reckoned to be the shortest way in time and effort. A waymarked path N from this hamlet (tarmac road access) ascends over scrubby pasture to join GR93 at pt.1460 in 1.3km. GR93 is then taken uphill without possible error to Col de Charnier (about 2h). Then as for the way described above (4h45 to summit).

ROCHER ROND   2453m

Costebelle slope. Possibly *the* classic ski outing of the area and certainly the most accessible and most rewarding of a series of E-slope Dévoluy runs. Usual best time, March/April according to snow cover (seal-skins and knives, ice axe optional). Much less pleasant in summer, as the Costebelle slope is covered with huge blankets of trackless scree.

From Agnières-en-Dévoluy by D317a to Lachaup hamlet, dominated by Rocher Rond – a bulky unexciting-looking mountain.   First go over treeless stone and boulder slopes. Ascent route on ski in uphill mode is quite obvious, WNW up the Chourum de la Combe des Buissons. The broad and inviting Costebelle snow flank is now tackled, keeping R(N) as much as possible before making a gradual ascending traverse SW to pt.2309 where there is one short steep section. Now working due W up plain slopes, the rounded summit is so reached (3h-3h30 from Lachaup).

All the effort put into this ski ascent is somehow seen in its proper perspective as one contemplates prepared slopes and chairlifts above the Joue-du-Loup resort, in full view opposite to the E. Seen at close quarters to the NNE, Grand Ferrand is most striking in winter raiment. The descent is a quality skirun, in particular most satisfying over the section between 2300-1700m. Lower down softer snow may make for hard work, a reminder that the time limit for starting the descent is roughly 10am, subject to conditions.

– o –

Crête des Baumes circuit 1720m

Recommended. The most popular summer walk from Super-Dév, affording widespread views over the area. Before the last vast carpark area at the resort, a signposted unmade lane at pt.1496 forks R(N). To its L a track skirts tennis courts and further N goes round a pony trekking stable in a patch of trees to rejoin lane beyond the plain Abert building. Shortly reach a crossroads at pt.1519. Turn L and follow large footpath WNW into pleasant grassy clearings and open forest, ignoring L and R turnings, up to the Collet du Tat (1613m), signpost, etc (30 min). Cliffs round the corner facing W offer numerous practice rock climbs.

To the N, go up grass and stones into stunted woodland and find a small but continuous winding trace; this trends R(NE) to exit on grass terraces. Work back L to main summit, 1720m (20 min). Splendid outlook.

Continue NE along broad back of Crête des Baumes, grassy lawns and limestone glacis, turning low humps generally keeping L near the edge. After one km the ground narrows to a ridge, and a small path appears as woodland fringes the crest. Go down the forested ridge over spot height 1518 (clearly a misprint for 1618 on TOP25 #3337 0T map), losing nearly 100m in height, until a track appears on the R, slanting back S; beware of a couple of smaller paths sighted before this (25 min). Follow track, contouring then descending gradually through the forest for one km and joining a higher track just before reaching the Boucherac bed near pt.1534 (signpost). Continue along large forest track to pt.1519 where the outward lane is encountered (45 min). Round trip, 2h-2h15.

Mère-Eglise at Gicon with the Obiou in background.

COL DE RABOU 1892/1888m

One of the major passes of Dévoluy, situated at its SE corner, and a key point for communications with the Buëch and Gapençais districts. Also an interesting coign of vantage for ramblers, though unfortunately disfigured by a TV relay station, while in summer backpacking traffic along GR94, which crosses the col, may be offputting. For access, see Accommodation section above, especially St-Etienne and Les Auches gîte and campsite.

Some 2.5km along D17 road after Les Auches, at crossroads just after Pont du Villard (1352m), take Bois Rond forestry track SE (motorable, picnic sites further up) to beyond first zag. Leave track near pt.1429 and follow a path SE that soon swings E under shoulder 1547m before returning SE and ascending over meadows to reach Jas de Barges shelter (1696m). Here, join GR94A (waymarks) heading SE; it tackles an easy outcrop and passes various Souloise springs before arriving at the col (2h45 from road). An alternative way takes a track directly E from Pont du Villard, with substantial shortcuts for pedestrians across wide bends of the track, up to Replat du Piocel (1562m), where GR94 is joined and followed to Col de Rabou in much the same time.

Note: N of the col, traces slanting across grass, scree and through rocks, can be followed at length and without difficulty to the highest point of the Raz de Bec (N peak, 2431m) in 2h (1h15 in descent).

MÈRE EGLISE, GICONS 1166m

One of the most spectacular and certainly the oldest monument in Dévoluy, though it is not fully clear whether of 11th century vintage, or built some time in the 13th. A typical example of a certain type of Romance-style church, of which there are numerous specimens in the Pré-Alps. Quite unmistakable because the main building is surmounted by a massive steeple more than half as high again as the structure on which it rests. What makes the Mother-Church at Gicons such an arresting sight is its location. Whereas other similar edifices are surrounded by houses, this one stands in splendid isolation atop a knoll above St-Disdier, visible for miles around.

Easily accessible on foot from St-Disdier-en-Dévoluy. In the little square by latter's town hall, nearby signpost indicates the: Mère-Eglise 30 min. Go up zigzags path with red/white flashes of GR93, passing 11 crosses just as if you were a medieval *chemin de croix* penitent. Surrounded by a low stonewall, the churchyard has freshly tended graves; the name Sarrazin is as common round here as Jones in a Welsh cemetery (25 min).

Vallon des Aiguilles   1800m

A fine hanging valley of meadows and springs situated on the GR94 Tour du Dévoluy, with optional approach from W, by Col des Aiguilles (qv), or E from Col du Festre (1442m), described below. There might be one bus a day across this pass.

In summer the route is absolutely simple, along GR94 from Col du Festre (signposts), past Serre Noir and small larch wood to mount somewhat steeper slopes to shoulder pt.1742m. Make a traverse above rockband to avoid the Saute Aure waterfall. Emerge on some of the finest upland pasture of the region, extending for 2km in direction of Col des Aiguilles (2005m); this pass is attained by the same waymarked path (2h45).

Vallon des Aiguilles is famous for its chourums, especially the one halfway up to N of path (indicated on TOP25 map), which was thoroughly explored 1962-1972 by potholers from Gap who managed to reach a depth of -980m.

PIC DE BURE   2709m

Hulking, sprawling giant, actually the culminating point of a whole group constituting the main outwork of the Dévoluy fortress on its S side, including the Montagne d'Aurouze, Plateau de Bure and Montagne de Barges. Conspicuous especially from Aspres-sur-Buëch when it reveals a daunting prospect of interminable scree slopes worthy of a Moroccan High Atlas summit. The E side of this massif reveals one of the most startling rockfaces in the French Alps, about 700m high in places and guaranteed to satisfy the most demanding big-wall contender. Moreover, a maze of rugged ridges interspersed with debris-filled gullies are sent out to all points of the compass. With snow lingering to June, the environment remains alpine till early summer, so mountain boots and ice axe are indispensible. In fact, apart from the normal route, the presence of snow warrants inclusion of a classic ski-touring itinerary.

Normal route. From the outskirts of Super-Dév (1504m), follow red/white flashes of GR94B footpath up through Bois d'Aurouze (larch), under the Jas chairlift (sometimes operates in summer), then along Prélourenq skitow over very stony ground, and beyond to pt.2076; route quite obvious so far. Path goes on to skirt Vallon Pierra de St-Etienne on R(W) side, winding upwards over scree to the breach of Sommarel (2375m), also reached by skitow of same name. Next section may be a little tricky in June due to presence of snow; otherwise (July-September) the path zigzags up the steep slopes to Brèche du Pic Ponson (2500m), cutting through rocks near the top with one fairly exposed part equipped with a cable (3h30-4h).

Now on the Bure plateau, head E across the broad expanse where génépi is found in season, to a national observatory; such is the percentage of sunny days up here that this scientific station has been built at 2564m. Scientists reach the plateau by means of a cableway to which ordinary mortals are denied access. Continue E on the level for some way to where others bound for the summit may be seen as they emerge from the Veynes (S) side, out of the depths of Combe d'Aurouze. From the saddle so reached, go ESE up gentle shale slopes (slippery in autumn after first snows) to summit (2h15, 5h45-6h15 from Super-Dév). Stupendous view N to Mont Blanc; S beyond Céüze to Montagne de Lure; W to the Cévennes, and E to mountains on the Italian frontier.

The return trek by same route entails some 4h30, so a full day is needed for successful accomplishment of this outing. A fast and fit party could doubtless save an hour or more.

Warning: In mist or whiteout conditions, avoid committing party to the featureless Bure plateau, guarded by sheer drops on all sides. Do not attempt a shortcut from the Petit Collet by going down N into Combe de Bure; you will be brought up sharply on the edge of a rockband halfway down. However, Combe Rattin (see below), under the Observatory, might provide a reasonably safe alternative.

Combe Rattin (on ski)

An energetic way of reaching the Plateau de Bure on foot and on ski by a decidedly alpine route. This description is based on conditions met in early May 1992, when knives, seal skins and ice axe proved invaluable.

Approach from St-Etienne-en-Dévoluy, initially along D17 serving the Super-Dév resort until Pont du Villard (1352m) is attained. Turn L up an unmade road that circulates through the Bois Rond coniferous forest - one of the few areas of woodland in this part of the massif. Pass a cool spring and reach spacious parking area with picnic site and shelter (Cabane d'Avalanche), pt.1534. Strike up grassy slopes S, with a rough path in an avalanche clearing, to exit from the tree-line at 1700m; large sheep-pen (1702m) is visible on L. Now zigzag over broken ground with steep grassy slopes and short rockbands to foot of outlying buttress of Corne (2111m); snow encountered from 1900m.

Having put on skins, climb steep broad combe between the Corne and Coste Belle ridge, levelling out after a few hundred m, till pt. 2048 is reached. In the immediate foreground slopes dip into large

116

hollow of Denflairar (to which access is also feasible via Combe and Vallon de Corne from the Bure plateau cableway bottom station above l'Enclus hamlet). Without losing too much height make a descending traverse L along fairly steep snow slopes beneath the Plate Longe cliffs to circumvent Denflairar hollow. At the foot of Tête de Chau (2521m), start a series of zigzags, still bearing L, up steepening slopes of avalanche snow. Imperative not to slip at this point as a long rockband lines foot of slope; fortunately this section is not technically difficult. Eventually emerge on the kinder slopes of Combe Rattin proper; the headwall of this cwm, crowned with the Observatory, rises into view. Go up in the bed making zigzag traverses on steep slopes till the summit plateau is attained. Allow 4h from picnic site.

In May, arrival on the plateau should be timed to allow for a halt, followed by switching ski to downhill mode. Start descent no later than 10.30am. Initial turns into Combe Rattin are euphoric, but negotiating avalanche slope (crust + large snowballs) above Denflairar requires jump turns and/or caution. Removing ski and gingerly descending over 100m or so, ice axe in hand, and pride in pocket, is totally acceptable. The remainder of the descent is straightforward.

Vallon Froid (on ski)

Montagne de Barges (Sommet de la Plane, 2316m) is a satellite of Pic de Bure and extends ENE towards Col de Rabou. Between two N-thrusting ridges lies a sheltered cwm - aptly named Vallon Froid - something of a ski tourer's dream come true. Its privileged location guarantees excellent quality snow even late in the season, making it the ideal May-morning 'quickie'.

From pt.1534 parking area (as for Combe Rattin above), follow GR94A, ESE through the Bois Rond to an intersection (1619m). Turn R(S) up branch that eventually goes past Fontaine des Corbeaux (1691m) and up path to Châlet du Vallon d'Ane. Continue ascending into Vallon d'Ane, gradually working SSW to tackle the headslopes at top of cwm; finish by making a rising traverse L to attain saddle S of pt.2019, between Vallon d'Ane and Vallon Froid (about 2h30 from Bois Rond parking area). The ideal descent takes skier down L-hand side of Vallon Froid to reach the forest road a couple of bends below Fontaine des Corbeaux.

– o –

GARGAS 2208m

Highly recommended. The best known – though not the highest – top of the little district of **Beaumont**, tucked away in a S corner of Isère, between Valjouffrey and the upper Drac. A friendly bit of country with softly rounded hills, fine woods, numerous meadows, and a whole cluster of little villages centred on **Corps** and the Route Napoleon (numerous hotels, gîtes). Chiefly famous because of **Notre–Dame de la Salette** (1770m), a large monastery which commemorates a memorable day. On 19 September 1846 the Virgin Mary, it is stated, appeared to a young shepherd, Maximin, and a shepherdess named Mélanie. She begged them to convey to their fellow villagers a lengthy message in French, and in Provençal, exhorting Christians to greater Godliness. Once word got round, the site became a focal point for pilgrimages, and the present large monastery was erected, together with many substantial outbuildings.

Initially pilgrimages were made on foot from St–Michel–en–Beaumont via the Col d'Hurtières, but nowadays people avail themselves of an excellent metalled road D212, winding but taking big coaches, that climbs from Corps. Now a regular institution, with enormous parking areas, curiosity shop, dining hall where visitors may have lunch, post office, programmed 'retreats' enabling harassed city–dwellers to indulge in theological discussions with the local priests, etc. Gargas is ascended from here; bus service from Corps.

Opposite main porch of monastery, facing the mountain, is a small monument depicting Our Lady with 2 shepherds. Just below on L, is a large footpath leading off L then R to a series of zigzags climbing N to gain the Col de l'Eterpat (1954m). Shortly before the grassy pass the main path slants L up the E ridge flank (not on crest), and mounts with regular steepness to summit cross and orientation table (1h30 or less). Fine view of Oisans and Dévoluy. Either go back the same way or traverse the mountain for more interest. Go along W ridge, narrow at first with a vague trace and exposed bits over rocks above engaging cliffs, to a promontory where the ridge broadens. Descend steep rock and grass slope to a large shelf running NW. Ignore this; go down grass slopes W/WSW, getting steeper and steeper; broken rock in parts needs route finding and care, all pathless, for 175m until the slope relents on the plain of Col d'Hurtières (1827m) where GR50 is joined. Now follow latter along large path SE/E back to monastery (1h15).

ooking back along W ridge to summit of Gargas.

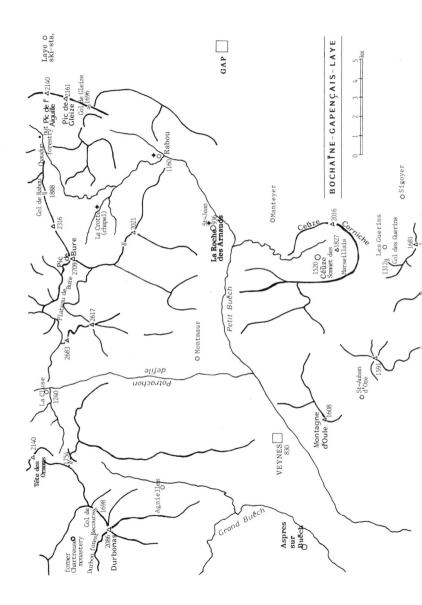

Laye O
ski-sta.

GAP

BOCHAÏNE – GAPENÇAIS – LAYE

0 1 2 3 4 5 Km

Col de Rabou· Chaudun Toresstry △2140
1888   Tuf Pic de l'   △2161
           Aiguille
Pic de △2161
Gleize   Col de Gleize
         1696

△2316

Pic △   La Crotte
Bure 2709   (chapel)

Plateau de Bure   △2021

2683 △ △2617
△
2140   O Rabou 1160

La Crotte
(chapel)

St-Jean
La Roche O △1996
des Arnauds

Celbze △2016
        Corniche
O Manteyer

Cébze △1827
Sommet des
1520 O Marseillais
Céüze

Petit Buëch

O Montmaur

1312 ‖ Les Guerins
        O Les Guerins
        Col des Guerins △1681

O Sigoyer

La Cluse
△1240
Potrachon défilé

△1591
O St-Auban
  d'Oze

Tête des Ormeas △2140
△1754

Montagne △1608
d'Oule

VEYNES
△830

former
Chartreuse O
monastery
Col de
Durbon forest Recourt
△1698

Agnielles
O

△2086

Durbonas

Grand Buëch

Aspres
sur
Buëch O

CHAMPSAUR

One of the oldest regional names, going back to Roman times: campus saurus = yellow field, and emphasises the agricultural aspect of this fine strip of country between Oisans and Dévoluy. Eons ago retreating Ice Age glaciers left vast alluvial deposits which have proved, together with a climate that is sunny without excessive dryness, eminently suitable to all forms of traditional agriculture. These broad open expanses of field and pasture beneath a peerlessly blue sky are a sight to gladden the heart of a traveller arriving from the Grenoble area, where he may have had fog and/or pollution to contend with. Col Bayard (1248m), that separates Champsaur from the Gapençais proper, is very much a climatic divide, though the saddle itself, crossed by a fast road, is hardly discernable on the ground.

Although embracing the whole upper Drac basin, upstream from the Beaumont district, for our purposes only that part of Champsaur lying between the N85 and the E limits of Dévoluy are detailed here.

Shortly after leaving Corps the Route Napoleon enters the department of Hautes-Alpes - Les Alpes vraies (the genuine Alps) the posters scream at you. If weary of hurtling along the N85, a side trip of no distance by roads along W side of the Drac will pay dividends. Rustic peoples cling to the land below the austere E ramparts of Dévoluy; visit what's left of Lesdiguières' great castle near Le Glaizil, a mournful sight - one can only hope that some local historical society will attempt to restore these crumbling walls as a fitting tribute to one of the greatest figures of Dauphiné.

An excellent base centre for those with a car intent on climbing Gargas (see previous entry), Pic de Gleize (see below), and generally for any walks in this district, is the comfortable gîte d'étape at Les Paris homestead, above Lallée village and the big bend in N85 near St-Firmin, about 15km SE of Corps and 20km NW of Col Bayard, N85. Inexpensive, self-catering in fully equipped kitchen, or meals provided by family. Along the N85, heading S, one will observe the D17 that climbs away R(W) and over the often closed Col du Noyer (1664m) with its crazy hairpin turns to reach St-Etienne-en-Dévoluy. The next sizeable village on the main road N85 to the S is Laye.

Laye (1300m), village and resort. One of those places that has tried to capitalize on an ideal location with all-year-round possibilities, and a large volume of tourist traffic. In summer there are long walks through the forested slopes of Pic de Gleize (2161m) and its tooth-shaped neighbour further N, Pic de l'Aiguille. A short way off is an 18-hole golf course, and nearby are tennis courts and equestrian activities.

In winter Laye functions as a medium size resort with 8 skilifts and a variety of woodland runs between 1900-1300m under the Pic de Gleize for all categories of skiers. Nordic skiing extends as far as the neighbouring resort of Col Bayard. In the last week of January an international meet is organised for sledge-dogs. Further details from local Syndicat d'Initiative (92.50.50.44).

PIC DE GLEIZE 2161m

Highly recommended. Superbly placed vantage point at the SE end of Dévoluy with all-embracing views of Champsaur, Oisans and Gapençais. Readily accessible from Laye on N85, turning off just N of Col Bayard and motoring some 4km to Col de Gleize (1696m); ample parking space. Picnic site.

Locate good path by going round E boundary of forester's lodge (inside the perimeter, dog and kennel) and ascend zags in scree and bushes N to emerge on large area of pasture; lots of cows in 1992. Continue N to a sharp bend L and go across steep slope to wind up R (N again) into a hollow with a few pine trees (note the S ridge directly above). Now follow narrow trenches in grass then stones almost due N, under the craggy E face of the mountain (not evident from map). Continue still with a good path trending slightly L to a little grass saddle some distance N of summit; tantaalising view of Pic de l'Aiguille further N. Now ascend main ridge S with increasing steepness to turn a forepeak on R, cross a gap and go on in a few paces to main top (1h30-2h).

South ridge alternative. Much more sporting, recommended. From the point indicated above, mount roughly over grass and rocks to crest and follow this steeply and with no path, turning obstacles generally on L side (about the same time).

On W side of Col de Gleize is the Chaudun forestry preserve (road unmade and chained off), a natural wildlife sanctuary on an abandoned village site where Corsican mouflon have been doing well since they were introduced into the district. Hence a mouflon's head adorns Laye resort's main signposts and take-away stickers.

Gleize on ski. January/April. Skitows from the Laye winter resort reach up through the woods to 1750m on E side of mountain. Depending on snowcover, leave a car either 500m from Col Bayard,

122

or at a hairpin pt.1483 on Col de Gleize road. Head NW up a broad
gully, leaving woods of larch and pine on R, where skitows end.
Work up a steepening slope for some 150m to a terrace area. Follow
this SSW to join line of summer route by going over a little ridge
near pt.1996 to enter the section through trenches; so along to
little saddle and summit ridge 2h/3h depending on start point and
conditions.

Pic de l'Aiguille 2140m

From little grass saddle on N side of Pic de Gleize (qv), follow the
narrow ridge N over pt.2106, 2105 with minor incidents, though
exposed and needing care (30 min). The E face is marked by two
prominent ribs and big dividing gullies of variable rock, overlooking the Laye woods and ski grounds. A number of 300m rock climbs
have been made here dating back to 1929.

BOCHAÎNE/GAPENÇAIS

An area that covers most of the W half of Hautes-Alpes, essentially in the immediate vicinity of Gap, the Petit Buëch valley to its source, and the main Buëch from Serres to St-Julien-en-Bochaîne, together with the Céüze/Barcillonnette massif.

Gap. This prefecture of 32,000 souls is the unrivalled capital of the S Alps. With its mountain-girt location, absence of pollution and generally fine weather (sunshine on at least 300 days a year) it compares more than favourably with Grenoble. Winding down from Col Bayard, the first view of Gap is that of a pleasant, harmonious town singularly lacking in high-rise monstrosities, depressed localities and other inescapable modern urban afflications. While being frequently occupied in the past by invading armies and, at times, partly destroyed, the town centre has retained much of its old-world charm; even more so as it is now a traffic-free shopping precinct through which one can stroll at leisure. Other places of interest are a museum containing the Lesdiguières mausoleum, a 19th century cathedral, a town library and local archives. All main services, various classes of hotels, 2 gîtes, B & B, etc. Local mountain information from the CAF (92.51.55.14). Tourist office and Bureau des Guides in July/August (92.51.57.03/92.53.60.75).

Bochaîne excursion bases

The name derives from the two Buëch rivers: Grand Buëch coming down from La Jarjatte in the Lus syncline, and Petit Buëch which springs from the S flank of Pic de Bure and joins the Grand Buëch at Serres. Thus, Bochaîne (and not Beauchêne as it is sometimes simplistically spelled) is the 'land of the Buëch' (from Latin, buchium or bochium).

It is an area of great variety – a kind of halfway house between Diois/Dévoluy massifs to the N and the Baronnies/Digne Pré-Alps to the S. While most of the streams drain S, the high ground occurs in N-S ridges descending from Dévoluy, giving way to a jumble of synclines and E-W oriented ridges. Climatically one of the most pleasant areas of France. Serres has 16 snow-days per year and 820mm rainfall, but it can freeze upwards of 100 days with generally clear skies and frequent bright spells between precipitation. Habitation is chiefly on *adret* slopes for protection from the bitter N wind. Architecture is similar in its simplicity to that of Trièves, farmhouses sporting typical pounti-style porches on stone pillars.

124

A plunging birth-rate is the obvious corollary to an ageing population and climbing death rate.

Veynes 830m, population about 3300, is arguably the chief town of the Bochaîne area. As a once important railway junction and engine repair shop it has had its heyday, while a large number of railworkers kept the pot boiling on the Union front; so much so that this bastion of the CGT (France's most influential union) was often known as Veynes la Rouge. Now very much in decline, and with ever diminishing passenger services, Veynes station platform signs announcing 'Veynes-Dévoluy' appear bombastic. Rail travel to Gap via Veynes is the subject of wisecracks in Grenoble, just as in Britain people joke about British Rail. The town is now waking up and concentrating on fruit, solar energy and tourism related activities. Among the latter should be mentioned gastronomy. There are several good restaurants; we can recommend Relais de la Poste, a Gault-Millau approved establishment with a minimum menu of 100Fr (92.57.22.25). An interesting development is a farm run by Christiane Giudicelli (92.57.25.47) that rears lamas for use as pack animals by ramblers. At nearby Montmaur castle, chilly though prestigious B & B accommodation is provided at 400Fr for two. Further information is available from tourist office (92.57.27.43).

Serres 670m, at the Buëch confluent, is a huddle of ancient buildings housing about 1200 people. Like nearby Aspres it has mostly retired folk who take advantage of the generous sunshine and sheltered location. Serres functions as a staging point with quality restaurants targeting motorized visitors; tourist office for information (92.67.00.67). Some buildings are of historic interest in connection with the religious wars of late 16th century; at one time Lesdiguières made Serres his chief citadel. The town has a camp ground but is otherwise of scant interest to the mountain walker. A little to the N, furnished accommodation is available at Aspremont (720m); Le Moulin (92.58.65.09). Also at Aspres-sur-Buëch (860m); La Chapelle (92.58.60.30).

All the abovenamed places are situated on the main railway line; this includes **St-Julien-en-Bochaîne** (922m), a somewhat lonely locality surrounded by steep hills, and with a slightly more severe climate. It has the roadside Hôtel des Alpins and 2 similar inns, plus a rural gîte at the Hameau des Oches (92.58.02.96). Sale of wool rugs is the chief tourist-oriented activity here; also this is a strategic staging point on the GR94E trail.

Céüze. Ambitiously denominated Céüze-Gap 2000. A basin of syncline, open on its N side, ringed with rockbands from NE to S and only 10km SW of Gap. Much frequented by skiing, walking,

N end of Céüze Corniche.

rock climbing and para-gliding exponents. The resort, situated on tree line at 1520m, has a hotel, a bistro or two, furnished accommodation, ski hire and instructors for winter sports December to April, après-ski entertainment and a tracked vehicle for transporting visitors up pistes to the summit corniche. About 9 skitows and runs of up to 500m are available.

Summit ridge is accessible to ski tourers. Park one km from resort at large bend near dog-kennel (chenil), cross Montmeyer torrent and climb through undergrowth, then up open slopes, heading E till crest is reached. Follow crest to pt. 2016 (1h45). The walking option is plainly more rewarding, with a choice of 2 routes in late spring and summer, and without the resort crowds of winter. Bus service from Gap.

Céüze Corniche 2016m

From S. Some 15km S of Gap on the N85 Route Napoleon, just short of Gap-Tallard aerodrome, go off along the D219 to Guérins hamlet (1275m) below col of same name; space for parking cars. Take GR94 which zigzags through forest to attain a path contouring at c1650m below Les Scies (1862m) on the Céüze rim. Leave GR on R, turn L(W) and walk up easy path in a gently ascending traverse till the escarpment is reached at c1720m. Work R(E) across moderate slopes of pt. 1862, then follow rim right round cliff edge to culminating pt. 2016 (2h30).

From N, as from the resort; more mundane. From Gap, leave the D994 at Roche des Arnauds (936m), follow the D18 to the S past Les Allemands and take hairpin turns up through mixed forest with fine views SE over deep gorge and boldly upthrusting Céüze escarpment; a few scattered chalets and small farms. On arrival in resort, spacious carpark in shade of coniferous forest. Go up Crête des Marseillais, to top station of skitow, called Sommet des Marseillais (1827m). From here head SE then E till summit is gained (1h45-2h).

Accommodation is possible during winter season at the resort; full pension at Hotel Gaillard (92.57.80.42). At Les Allemands, the Agapanthe gîte takes skiers in winter/spring, but caters more for equestrian visitors in summer (92.57.91.51). At La Roche des Arnauds there is a perfectly adequate roadside inn.

Col de Rabou 1892/1888m

From S (May to September). The N approach is described in the Dévoluy section. Coming from the S, this key Dévoluy col is more strenuous than from the N. Access is from La Roche des Arnauds by D513/503 along pine-studded W flank of Bois du Devès (1504m)

14th century church at Rabou hamlet.

Pic de Bure E pillar from path junction pt. 1382 near Rabou.

ridge; narrow but recently resurfaced. Picturesque itinerary with views into Petit Buëch gorge, and Rabou hamlet (1150m) with 14th century church crowning a prominent spur. Ample parking space. Irregular community bus.

Go on up by GR93/94, past an oratory dedicated to St-Rosaline (1195m), then turn L(NW) along the Sentier des Bans hacked out from horizontal strata for over 3km. Waymarking indicates that after another cross (1268m) one leaves GR93 and follows GR94 down to ford the Petit Buëch (bridge often swept away). Ascend the opposite bank, crossing ruins and evidence of former fields up to ruined hamlet of Les Berthaud (1133m), 1h15.

Continue E up Vallon de la Crotte, crossing vestigial fields to Chapelle de la Crotte (1310m) at edge of woods. This is the site of the former Berthaud monastery (1188-1448), of which nothing remains apart from a ruined 12th century Romance chapel. A more recent building nearby still attracts pilgrims on 29 June. The GR94A crosses Torrent de la Crotte, briefly heads E to circumvent Crête de la Lauze, then swings back N in a rising traverse of ensuing wooded slope (Clot Mollet); beyond this emerge onto scree slopes. Far above, and to the L(NW), loom the tops of Montagne des Barges. Now go up by a stone chute to foot of cliff barring approaches to the col (2h30 from Les Berthaud).

By a giddy ledge trail beneath an overhanging face, work carefully upwards to the R with a couple of tricky places, coming out onto grassy slopes that reach the col without further incident. Formerly used by mules, now rarely frequented except by walkers, this bit of the route requires the utmost caution (30 min, 4h15 in all from Rabou).

Well worth the effort, as the views obtained make this one of the finest sights in the area, especially when late spring snow still decorates the upper bastions. One gazes across the wild rugged S side of Dévoluy - deep-cut gorges dominated by steep forested slopes, and the majestic E face of Pic de Bure.

– o –

EXCURSIONS FROM VEYNES

MONTAGNE D'OULE 1608m

Recommended. The most easily accessible of the summits S of the Veynes-Gap highway, thanks to the superb waymarking of GR94D, this top belongs to the remote Céüze/Barcillonnette massif. Leave Veynes centre by the D648 and head S to cross the Petit Buëch bridge, pt.809; the GR is signposted on the other side of the road.

Go up to Haute Morelle farm, heading SSE. Beyond farm, the path loops back R(SW), then resumes a SE course up through forest to attain Col d'Oule (1397m, 2h). From here follow easy ridge due W to summit (45 min, 2h45 from Veynes). Splendid vantage point.

Other tops of interest in this massif, also served by variants of GR94, are **Montagne d'Aujour** (1834m), some distance S, a well forested locality with an artificial lake. The double-crested ridge of **Crête des Selles** (1386m) just S of Barcillonnette, from which it may be reached by a forest road. And another fine basin of syncline, the **Montagne de St-Genis** (1492m), further S still and done from Savournon (720m).

Chazal meadows from La Cluse

Access from Veynes to La Cluse (1241m) by the D937 road to the Col du Festre (bus). A short walk up into the E-facing combe between the 2 Garnesier Aiguilles. From La Cluse follow a track due W along Abéou torrent, initially with red/white waymarks of GR94D. At a fork in one km keep R(NW) to reach ruined sheep pens at Voran (c1300m). Go on up more or less parallel with the Abéou torrent to your L, passing under power lines and rounding a rib to reach the Chazal barn. Now head W through beech, past Rocher de la Baume (1647m), keeping on across the meadows of a gentle plateau to attain pt.1779 on ridge that descends from Roc Garnesier (2383m), which, with its sister peaks, dominates the the scene throughout the excursion (1h30-2h from La Cluse).

D U R B O N A S   2086m

A SW outlier of the Dévoluy massif, this pine covered mountain is the highest point in Bochaîne. A grand vantage point with fine views NE of Grand Ferrand, Garnesier, Montagne d'Aurouze, and S to Céüze, Montagne de Lure and Ventoux. It demands a a slightly strenuous forest hike via road, track and path, marked with red/white GR94 flashes to the Recours col (1698m) followed by ridge wandering through occasionally dense forest. Ski-pole and/or ice axe essential in winter.

From the N75 at St-Julien-en-Bochaîne (922m, bus), a small metalled road NE serves forestry hut and holiday camps of the Bouriane valley. Private vehicles cannot go beyond the bridge at L'Etroit (1.5km, padlocked barrier, no access sign), contrary to statements in other guidebooks saying that vehicles may reach former Chartreuse monastery of Durbon.

After crossing the bridge, tramp the road alongside stream; altnatively follow GR94E flashes above L side of stream and road, past forestry hut. Halfway up the valley, buildings of the Pré Mulets holiday camp are seen in a clearing. The valley is thickly wooded with fir, pine and beech; some evidence of new plantations and attempts to stabilize streambed. Former Chartreuse Durbon monastery (1210m, now a holiday camp) is situated where metalled road ends (4.5km, 1h15).

Now follow prominent GR94C flashes up path SE that cuts corners of forest track before finally leaving it and striking directly for Recours col up steepening inclines. Path crosses Combe-Longue logging road for the last time. Signpost marked 'Durbonas' indicates alternative path leading W through forest. Follow steep path through trees to grassy col set amid dispersed pines (1h).

Head SW along ridge of forested knolls, working round L(S) to outflank outcrops, and emerge on spacious open saddle. Final wooded and apparently steep heights of Durbonas are now in view. Cross another wooded knoll, then dip down to the Leschaup pass (1750m). Strong evidence of game in the vicinity; hare and black grouse droppings, chamois and red deer hoof marks, bark chaffed by stags' antlers, etc.

Now wind up moderately steep wooded slopes, gradually bearing L(S) to come out on the E/SE ridge whence summit is visible again. Progress up this ridge is easier than going up directly SW in the forest; in winter it is mostly snow-free. Impressive views S down steep slopes to head of Agnielles valley. Angle eases off as flattish summit is reached (1h30 from Recours col, 3h30 from the Etroit bridge, 3h45-4h from St-Julien). Return the same way (2h30).

TOUSSIÈRE 1916m

Elegant tapering pyramid and pastoral mountain composed of contrasting steep slopes of grass and stone cut by shelving ledges and rockbands. The most prominent summit on the long N-S watershed after Jocou and beyond (S of) the Col de Grimone. Not as prestigious as Jocou but distinctly more satisfying; recommended. Situated on borders of the Diois/Bochaîne districts, it can be approached from 4 completely different directions. The route taken below is more of a serious mountain walking challenge than most of the other ways; the latter are appended briefly hereafter.

From East by ENE ridge. On the N75 going S, just after the second southerly turning E into Lus la Croix-Haute, take next turning R into La Caire hamlet (c990m, bus stop); parking possible on grass/gravel verge with local residents permission. Prominent signpost: Toussière-GR94. Initially take latter due W, along the broad earth/stone track up a wooded ravine, separated by wire fence from deeply entrenched stream, and beside fields where horses graze. In 15 min the track trends SW; prepare to leave red/white GR flashes (notice to this effect on tree), and bear R(NE) as for Col de Lus.

Now over open ground the path, waymarked with blue blobs and red/yellow flashes, follows close to Ruisseau de l'Etroit, into deciduous woodland; overgrown, ruined chapel formerly belonging to Knights Templars seen on R. As wooded ravine narrows, go straight up along more or less dry watercourse; in wet conditions make detour to R (instruction board on tree); main path and detour rejoin some 200m further on, and soon emerge onto slopes of a large clearing. Waymarks now become infrequent and path in grass not always visible until another woodland belt is penetrated. The gradient leads on up through forest to a col (c1280m) with long grass and dwarf pine (50 min). Just below this point the historic Chemin des Templiers arrives from the R (ENE). [The combined trail can be followed W and WNW for 2.5km across mainly wooded slopes to the Col de Lus (1497m), visible in the distance below Serre des Oeufs (1758m), a handsome sub-peak with fine conifers on its NE flank; see alternative way (1) below].

As col 1280m is reached, one final yellow arrow is observed aiming L(SW) in the direction of pt.1743 on ENE ridge. Ascend the pathless slope in this direction into timber and persevere with route finding through trees in the SW line till a large clearing is attained. Now zigzag up steepening slopes to a narrow band of deciduous trees. Once this has been crossed, the next grass slope is at 35°, much eroded by grazing and so criss-crossed by drailles as to afford step-by-step progress as going up a staircase. As the slope relents, unaccountably red/yellow flashes reappear and pt.1743 is thus reached; impressive view into N cwm of mountain, very much an alpine scene on this side with ENE ridge angling up nicely to summit above clumps of fir and inclined meadows; probably large flocks of sheep visible (1h10).

From pt.1743, descend slightly to broad saddle and go up sharp rocky ENE ridge. Follow faint intermittent red/yellow flashes adhering to a trod; avoid temptation to use drailles across gravel, steep tussocks and grass to R(NW) in order, inadvisably, to turn first ridge step. Go on with regular steepness to top; no cairn or bench mark; small 'borne' stone visible (45 min, 2h45 from La Caire). Proper mountain footwear is needed for this route and all the others noted below.

Descent by S/SE slopes. Easier on feet and legs than going down the ascent route. On S side of summit successive scree ledges

Toussière from pt.1743. ENE ridge on L, N ridge on R.

afford an easy line, interrupted by a few rocky steps - mud-splat-
tered from frequent use by sheep - leading to some gentle grassy
slopes. Head down S past drinking troughs and a ruined hut as
red/yellow flashes reappear. Still more or less due S, go down
comfortably to a shepherds' hut in good repair, usually occupied
in summer. A short way E is a big GR94 signpost indicating directions for Lus la Croix-Haute and Vaunières hamlet. Follow GR94
down across slopes E to Col des Oches (1480m). This saddle is
not named on some maps and lies under the headland of Roc Bernon
(1546m) (50 min). Continue by GR94, now NE, going down steeply
into deciduous forest along a path liberally sprinkled with horse
dung (pony trekkers). Lower down the trail is more vague as it
crosses open country to reach the first fields. A stream tinkles
unseen in bushes on the R. Soon reach the Col de Lus junction
(on ascent route) and the trail back to La Caire (55 min, 1h45 from
summit).

Alternative routes. (1) From col 1280m continue along Chemin
des Templiers to Col de Lus (1497m), as noted above (55 min, 1h45
from La Caire). Now climb the bold N ridge, traversing the intermediate distinctive Serre des Oeufs (1758m), 2 steep steps, vague
traces and quite exposed in places (1h30, 3h15 from La Caire).

(2) From **Vaunières** (1175m), below S side of mountain, access by
D210 country lane from the N75, about 6km S of the Lus turning.
This interesting and formerly abandoned hamlet was happily rev-
ived in 1964 by the Village des Jeunes association; gîte and modest
catering for visitors (92.58.15.54). From hamlet the easiest way
is by GR94, on the N leg to vicinity of new shepherds' hut just
above the Col des Oches, then to summit by reversing the descent
described above (2h30).   More serious and much finer, go along
the NW leg of GR94, over Col de Vaunières saddle (1419m) to well
marked fork about 400m distance short of Col Varaime (1447m).
Go off R (NE), still in woodland, by rapid zigzags up to bare rough
slopes leading over pointed top of La Pare (1862m), all waymarked,
to continue by a fine upland roof heading NE to summit (2h45-3h
from Vaunières).

(3) From W side.   Car essential, a frequented waymarked route
by GR94.   From Châtillon-en-Diois, SE through impressionable
lower branch of the Gas gorge by D539 to junction after a tunnel
with its upper branch, pt.663.   Go ahead SE along narrow D148
to outskirts of Boulc village.   Turn L(E) up a broken lane to road
head at Les Tatins hamlet (1150m). Prominent signpost: GR94-
Col Varaime-Toussière.   Follow this with a moderate gradient
over pasture and skirting the big Noir forest, up to col. Continue
for 400m to junction with path leaving GR94 and mounting NE in
summit direction, as for (2), about 3h from Les Tatins.

(4) From N, starting at Col de Grimone (easy roadside parking,
1318m), a big track/path S goes along pasture and woodland on
E side of main ridge to reach the Col de Lus (1497m) in 1h.   Then
as for route (1), total time 2h30.   The shortest way to summit.

B A N E   1643m

Significant summit on N side of the Valdrôme syncline, easily tackled from the D993 road running between Die and Aspres-sur-Buëch
(bus service).   Start at La Beaume village (890m) on D993; Hôtel
de la Poste (92.58.60.61).   Cross Valence-Briançon railway line
and the Chauranne stream and follow waymarked GR94E through
sparse oak forest into Les Bois Noirs.   The GR zigzags up flank
of Banillon (1437m), reaches the Clot Aubanel spring, traverses
beech and coniferous forest, skirts the Aup meadows and arrives
at the Fontaine de l'Aup (1528m), 2h15.   From here, gentle slopes
lead SW to summit in another 15 min.

Either go down the same way; or with transport available/bus
connection, follow ridge SW then NW in general direction of Col
de Cabre.   At 1400m level, a path coming in from Banillon to the

R(NE) is joined and makes for easier progress along to Col de Valdrôme (1304m). Path now heads NNW down through forest to Col de Cabre (1180m), inn and parking, on D993 (1h45 from summit, in ascent 2h15). From here a forest track winds up below the NW ridge and eventually reaches saddle behind the Banillon shoulder, to connect with ascent route; this is another alternative.

DRÔME - PROVENÇALE BORDERS

In this most southerly district of the ground covered in the present guide numerous indications appear that Provence is drawing closer. Olive trees are seen, vineyards, drier landscapes, bluer skies and higher temperatures. The hills start to sort themselves out of the appalling jumble they had got into in the Diois/Bochaîne region. From N–S, the main orientation is angling round to NW–SE, with a tendency to produce isolated peaks in the W sector above Nyons, while N of the Eygues, near Rémuzat the main crest runs W–E, echoing the disposition of ridges in the Baronnies and Ventoux region further S.

This is one of the remotest areas of France, especially between La Motte Chalancon and Dieulefit; it is sometimes referred to as *le désert français,* depopulated last century and now struggling to make a comeback with sheep rearing and tourism. Here also we encounter the most northerly *villages perchés,* such as St–May which occupies a meander of the Eygues; and historically a stronghold of Protestantism. For accommodation and outdoor activities information contact various tourist offices: Dieulefit (75.46.42.49), Rémuzat (75.27.85.78), La Motte Chalancon (75.27.21.10).

Nyons 259m, pop.6300, is the chief town, situated at a point where the river Eygues exits from the hills. A pleasant locality with a congenial climate that makes it a favourite with tourists and retirees alike. Local resources: olive oil, fruit, jam and wine. Nyons is on the edge of the famed Tricastin plain and its various AOC wines (Valréas, Coteaux du Tricastin, Cote du Rhône Villages, etc). As you drive along the D538, vineyards on your R(NE) extend to the foothills of Montagne de Lance, with magnificent roadside roses whose purpose is to give wine-growers advance warning if blight is about to strike. Nyons information on phone 75.26.10.35. A car is needed to partake in most of the excursions described here.

MONT RACHAS 898m

One of the lowest tops described in this guide, a unique lookout platform over the Rhône valley and Nyons area at the W extremity of the Southern Pre-Alps. Really a wooded ridge with outcrops on its S flank rising above boar-haunted forests. Usually reached from Aleyrac by GR429, or from Taulignan or Dieulefit. The latter way can be done as a 4WD drive all the way to the summit. Our route entails more walking than driving.

After Grignan, the most secret lair in France for truffles, and visited for its historically famous castle which was a favourite vacation spot for Madame de Sévigné in the 17th century, follow the D14 and D538 up Lez valley to Roche-St-Secret (an enchanting name). In middle of village turn off L, just before a restaurant, along narrow metalled road that soon divides. Take the L-hand branch signposted: Serre Bourdon and Douit. Now on a driveable piste, go round to L of farm (sheep in spring and friendly sheep dog) over stony track that gets progressively steeper as it enters forest of oak, pine and juniper. The surface is bad 400m after the farm; park a vehicle here. At next fork, leave branch leading to beautifully restored house on R with swimming pool, and head L past another stone farmhouse beneath giant oaks with a sign: *Chemin privé avancez lentement.* This is for the benefit of trail bikes. In 1993 a vintage Peugeot 203 Estate was observed quietly rusting in adjoining garage.

Leave kitchen garden and small reservoir on R; path narrows as it climbs through genet bushes (gloriously blossoming end-May) to reach GR429 near an abandoned sheep pen by a large pine. Pig-wire fences off land beyond GR. Now strike L(W) along the track through oak, beech and maple, following red/white flashes, smooth and congenial at first, but becoming steep and rutted as it breasts the inclines leading to Col de la Croix (671m). Recently cleared forest openings are seen on L, while track descends slightly then climbs again as it veers out of sight to R.

After col, continue W for about 300m along to junction with prominent tombstone marked: *Pour notre ami André.* Here turn sharp R along a pleasant, unmarked path leading up gentle forest slopes towards Rochas summit; residual horse manure indicates riders use same path. Oak now more in evidence with random juniper and stunted pine; some of the last named is in poor condition. The path gets onto the ridge, now increasingly rocky; glimpses below of Roche-St-Secret and over to Montagne de la Lance. Small grassy pasture and vigorous boxwood bushes near summit adorned with TV relay. Good view N beyond Dieulefit to Saoù/Trois Becs massif (round trip of some 3h from farmhouse).

MONTAGNE DE LA LANCE 1338m

Traversed by GR9, an elongated NW-SE oriented forested ridge overlooking the Tricastin plain, and the last top of any consequence in the Southern Pre-Alps. Easy ascent to summit pastures, fringed on E side by the Rocher Garaux cliffs. Access from Nyons along D538 to turn-off R(E) just after Roche-St-Secret, and driving up D545, leaving ruins of a village perché (Béconne) on L. Follow narrow metalled road to an intersection, signpost, etc, where it is advisable to park a car.

A track with GR flashes goes up R past Maison Baume-la-Lance, leaving Montjoux path on L(N); continue to another intersection and head up into beech forest. Trend R above final house (Champ Rousset), going up a forest track purportedly out of bounds to all vehicles. Conifers appear and a sharp bend is reached at pt. 840. Now turn R(W), emerge from beech forest at a gate and keep on up track to pt. 979; now swing back SE as GR9 climbs through sparse, stunted pine over the hill's great hogsback to pt. 1259. The gentle walk continues (waymarks) all the way to the summit. Superlative view SW over Tricastin plain to Rhône valley; SSE to Ventoux; N to Diois; chance sighting of a chamois is possible (2h45-3h15).

MONTAGNE DE MIÉLANDRE   1451m

Access as for Angèle (see below), heading NW after St-Ferréol to Valouse col on S side of mountain. A handsome, sharply-defined summit seen to best advantage from D538 between Dieulefit and Bourdeaux. A pastoral top, much like adjacent Angèle, and remarkable in that the summit pasture contains a small spring. Park a car at Col de Valouse (735m), go up ENE towards sheep pen, then NNE along unmarked path (signpost: Miélandre) to cross Col de Portalier. Follow path R through woods to emerge on the upper meadows of Miélandre. Keep to a trod up grassy slope; after a cairn trend R to a shoulder, then head L to main top (2h45).

MONTAGNE D'ANGÈLE   1606m

One of the main tops of the Nyons massif, this writing-desk of a mountain features extensive summit pastures overlooking crumbling cliffs, steep scree, and scraggy deciduous forest on N side. Sometimes called *la porte de la Provence,* it is regularly frequented each summer by flocks of sheep. Hence dogs and motor bikes are forbidden while parties on foot and horseback are simply tolerated. The mountain is a superb vantage point with commanding vistas S to Mont Ventoux and the Montmirails; N to Col de Rousset, Grand Veymont and other landmarks of the Vercors, not to mention the summits of Dévoluy and snowclad giants of Oisans.

From Nyons follow meanders of the Eygues valley NE through pleasant, wooded, sparsely populated country with a profusion of olive and cherry trees. In 10km turn L at La Bonté up D70, past

Condorcet to a fork at the interesting village of St-Ferréol-Trente Pas; handsome church with campanile. Take R branch by D186; fields of lavender appear and further up occasional pear trees; reach crossroads at les Chaudrons (576m). Leave tempting-looking village atop a spur to L and go R up narrowing switchback road to Col de Chaudebonne (763m); fine view of Villeperdrix (partridge town) nestling in a hollow to SE. Continue by road now zigzaging N, unsurfaced (in 1992) over the last couple of km through stunted oak forest, with boxwood undergrowth, to a parking-slot some 50m from Brezil farmhouse (1140m), next to small spring. Farmer will probably not emerge with shotgun, but his 2 dogs are fairly aggressive.

Now go on foot up 'jeepable' private track (past usual noticeboard warning visitors about motorized trespass) that climbs R(N) from farmhouse, then twists and turns over the gently curving Chaudebonne hillside, till a fairly large sheep pen is reached at c1500m (1h15 from farm).

Now head up NNW towards the summit pastures, to the grassy dip between Rocher de l'Esqueyron and the Rocher de l'Aigle; view unfolds NNE to Vercors and Dévoluy, with the scattered hamlets of commune d'Arnayon at one's feet. This is where a rough path arrives from Meffre hamlet to the N (20 min from sheep pen). On a fine day the sky will be reasonably empty, except for an odd helicopter or plane on a training flight; you might see a pair of high wheeling buzzards, or a brace of ground-hugging sparrow hawks.

Work WNW up a shallow trough in summit pastures, gradually bearing R to reach a 'striding edge' W of Rocher de l'Esqueyron (1602m). Then follow yellow waymarks at irregular intervals, keeping short rockfaces to your R until culminating point, Rocher Merlu (1606m) is reached (30 min from Rocher de l'Aigle, 2h15 from Brezil farmhouse).

In descent, take a shortcut to reach one of the zags of 'jeepable' track some 300m WNW of above-mentioned sheep pen. However, avoid descending R too early because of a short rockband, some unpleasant vegetation and steep scree. This ground is typical habitat terrain for partridge; 3 were observed in 1992. Backpack travellers traversing limestone blocks some 200m from track will no doubt notice an inscription to the effect that someone called Auguste, and another called Peysson, died there in 1903. Whether from lightning, snake bite or surfeit of pastis is not specified.

Approaching Rocher Merlu summit of Montagne d'Angèle from E.

FRANCO - PROVENÇAL LEXICON

adret	*southern slope*
aup, alp	*mountain pasture*
avere	*basic resource, sheep*
bachal, bachasson	*drinking trough*
balme, baume	*cave, grotto*
bana	*horn*
bayassières	*lavender fields*
béou	*drinking place*
cabre	*goat*
cagnard	*stifling heat*
casse	*large scree slope*
chava	*horse*
châtel	*castle*
chourum	*limestone chasm*
clapier	*large blocks of stone*
claps	*scree/rock-slide*

clue, cluse	*gorge*
collet	*little col, pass*
collu	*small col, saddle*
coutil	*hollow*
cunillères	*primitive toilets between houses*
drailles, drayes	*contouring sheep trails*
ermes	*pasture*
essart	*field cleared by slash-and-burn*
glacière	*old snow in deep cavity*
ilamou	*up over there*
ilava	*down over there*
jalina	*hen*
jas	*sheep pen*
kalobrina	*salamander, snake*
kayou	*swine*
lapiaz	*limestone pavé*
lauzon	*locality of limestone slabs*
lyoura	*hare*
mainbou	*high inaccessible region*
mollard	*bluff, hill*
motte	*knoll, small hill*
moutella	*ferret*
olagnier	*willow*
orsière, oursière	*bear's habitat*
pertuis	*narrow pass/gorge(opening)*
picodon	*traditional goat cheese*
poët	*well (French = puits)*
pot	*circular hollow in limestone pavé*
pounti	*overhanging portion of roof*
raben	*ravine*
ratié, rattier	*kite, sparrow hawk*
rif	*stream*
riou	*torrent (sometimes dry)*
scialet	*limestone chasm*
serre, serriou	*long mountain ridge*
taisson	*badger*
ubac	*northern slope*
vachi, vatsi	*cow (French = vache)*
villard	*village*

PRINCIPAL ROCK CLIMBING SITES

VERCORS

Les Trois Pucelles 2km SE of St-Nizier-du-Moucherotte. Classic Grenoble local practice ground on 3-4 big pinnacles about 130m high, first explored in the 1920s but modern-style climbs were not made until the 1940s. The main routes, some 10 in number, are at least grade IV and most are much harder.

Les Bernards (Bec de Cornillon) 1.5km ESE of Lans-en-Vercors. Variety of hard practice climbs, some 70m long.

Presles Long high cliffband fringing N side of the Bourne gorge, stretching from above Choranche W-E for some 4km. First hard route was put up in 1953; there are now at least 50 climbs varying from 150-300m, mostly of grade V or harder.

Cournouse Opposite Presles escarpment on S side of the Bourne gorge, a salient massif where the main cliffs face W; explored in the 1970s, now with a dozen routes of IV+ to VI.

Gerbier The notable Prélenfrey section of the Vercors E escarpment, between Col Vert (N) and Pas de l'Oeille (S). The main 400m high cliff and its many routes commence from the N end proper at a feature called Double Brèche. The centre of this long wall was climbed by a meandering line to the summit (2109m) as early as 1927 (grade III+). Further routes were made in the 1950s, and many more in the 1960/70s. The most famous and one of the most popular climbs is the Arc-de-Cercle Crack (400m, V+); the last 80m consist of short vertical steps with a variety of grassy pitches of grade III/III+; it was here that the great French alpinist Lionel Terray, and his companion Marc Martinetti, fell to their deaths in September 1965. The main Gerbier ridge can be followed without exceeding grade II+, while on the W facet there are ways up of similar standard. The Sultane pillars, at the S end and on the W side, offer short, technically difficult climbs that can be reached in 45 min from the Côte-2000 cableway.

Deux-Soeurs Complex twin rockfaces on the escarpment S of the Gerbier section, and divided by the prominent Deux-Soeurs gully, described in the main text. Though now sporting numerous routes, all fail in interest against the magnificent SE Pillar (Spigolo) of Agathe (320m, V+), first accomplished in 1960 and one of the most sought-after climbs in Vercors.

Playnet Impressive rock architecture in this part of E escarpment consisting of 6-7 towers at pt.1994, above St-Andéol hamlet. A dozen routes of 250-300m graded IV+ upwards, dating from the early 1960s.

Parquet A stretch of the E escarpment facing Mont Aiguille, with summit pts.2024, 1931, 1945. Numerous routes of IV to VI, 250m, climbed since 1950, though most are technically serious.

Mont Aiguille The rock with the most kudos in the Vercors but not rated all that highly among climbers for routes of great interest or quality. The historical background and normal route are detailed in the main text. Note that the debatable alternative regular chimney route called the Tubulaires (IV) is now regarded as too awkward and unpleasant, and is only used as a partial line for an abseil descent. To its L is the most popular climbers' route, Voie des Gemeaux, mostly IV with short bits of IV+/V, 180m, which traverses into the Tubulaires exit pitches about two-thirds way up the face. The Coupé routes of 1953-58, on or near the S pillar, are among the best of the original modern and nowadays classic climbs on the rock (200m, V). About 50 climbs to date; some are grade VII.

Glandasse-Archiane Huge cirque terminating S end of Vercors plateau. Less popular than other Vercors sites because of long approaches (2-3h), especially the Glandasse climbs, not in the cirque at all and found on the N-S escarpment overlooking the Valcroissant abbey and Die to the W. Sections of this 450m discontinuous cliff, stretching from N of Rocher de Peyrole to the Roc d'Ambane at the S end, afford several serious challenges, some of which are multi-day enterprises, rarely assessed below grade V+ and with numerous artificial pitches. They include Rocher des Heures, Paroi de Glandasse, Le Pestel (a huge monolith), and the Ambane Pillar. The original climbs were done in 1961; as features they are so prominent as to be marked on the TOP25 map.

The Rocher d'Archiane projects into the centre-rear of the cirque with a cliff elevation of 400m. Climbs go back to 1951, but the conspicuous SE pillar edge of the Livanos route was not done until 1959 (V+); among half a dozen other routes, this remains the most frequented. More recently, other crags and pinnacles in the Archiane cirque have been climbed.

DIOIS

Trois Becs/La Pelle/Roche Courbe   The vicinity is described in text under Le Veyou.   The Voie des Parisiens original route (250m V+) retains a cachet unchallenged in the Vercors region.   The cliffs stretching above the Chaudière pass road, through the various salient features of La Pelle (1545m) and the Signal (1559m), now provide 2 dozen routes, some easier, some harder than the original climb, and of 350m.   With easy access, this climbing venue is currently as frequented as any other in this guidebook.   New routes (usually VI/VI+), some of doubtful merit and "splitting hairs", continue to be made every year so far in the 1990s.

DÉVOLUY

Obiou   General information is given in text.   The old (1927) NW face itinerary in zigzags for 500m remains the exemplary mountaineering way (II); it is rarely done today (6h30).   The E face route of 1940 (III/IV) is more direct than the normal route, is unfashionable, has complex route finding but finishes almost directly at summit (6-7h).   Modern routes, generally V, on the northern pillars are not often done.   The immense tabular formation of cliffs on this mountain does not lend itself to modern-style rock climbing.

Gillardes   Long cliff enclosing E side of the Souloise gorge below St-Disdier.   Numerous serious climbs of 450-550m, IV+/VI+, first reconnoitred by Georges Livanos in the 1960s.

Pic de Bure   Noted in text.   Though its huge NE cliffs were first explored in 1943, the great route by Desmaison on the L edge of this area, the E Pillar, outshines anything else in the neighbourhood.   500m, sections of V+, 26 pitches, remote.   Rarely climbed because of distant access, and when tackled it usually involves a bivouac on the pillar (good places) or on the descent.

Crête des Bergers   Noted in text.   Even more remote than Pic de Bure, a long complicated cliff with routes of 450m.   Several very serious climbs, usually V+/VI with artificial pitches.

SELECTED SHORT BIBLIOGRAPHY

Note. The author consulted and presented a list of over 60 works, and numerous articles from journals and magazines. The list has been reduced to a number of key historical volumes, works currently in print and others of value to French readers.

Barnola, P. & Faure, J. *L'Obiou*. Imp. Léostic, Gap, 1982

Bolle, P. *Grenoble et le Vercors: de la résistance à la Libération.* La Manufacture, Lyon, 1985

Coolidge, W.A.B.(Ed.). *Alpine Guide to the Western Alps, 4th Ed,* Longmans Green, London, 1898

Cordier, P. *Les Préalpes du Sud (100 Plus Belles Courses).* Denoël, Paris, 1988

Coupé, S. *Escalades en Chartreuse et Vercors (incl. Les Trois Becs), 2nd Ed.* Arthaud, Grenoble, 1972
  > *En Chartreuse et Vercors, escalades et randonnées.* Arthaud, Grenoble, 1977
  > *Escalades dans le Vercors.* Edisud, Aix-en-Provence,1993

Dalloz, P. *Vérites sur le drame du Vercors.* F. Lanore, Paris, 1979

Dreyfus, P. *Histoire de la Résistance en Vercors.* Arthaud, Grenoble, 1975

Dupont, M. *Le Guide du Vercors.* La Manufacture, Lyon, 1986

Ferrand, L. & Borrel, J. *Trièves, pays de La Mure.* Didier & Richard, Grenoble, 1989

Germain, F. *Escalades choisies-Tome II Alpes du Sud.* Arthaud, Grenoble, 1948

Isler, F. & Mingasson, C. *Randonnées dans la Drôme Provençale.* Edisud, Aix-en-Provence, 1993

Joanne guide. *Alpes Dauphinoises, Vol. 1.* Paris, 1890
  > *Dauphiné.* Paris, 1898

Meyzenq, C. *Hautes-Alpes, Ubaye, Haut-Drac, Préalpes Drômoises.* Ed. Ophrys, Gap, 1984

Perez, J. *Les Massifs du Gapençais.* Didier & Richard, Grenoble, 1982

Reymond, R. *La Route Napoléon, de l'Île d'Elbe aux Tuileries.* La Manufacture, Lyon, 1985

Various GR guides issued by FFRP/CNSGR Paris for combinations of *GR9, 91, 93, 94, 946, 95 etc. Especially note: Tours dans les Hautes Alpes du Sud, GR94/946.* Paris, 1986.

Later editions of some of the works listed above may have been issued for date-lines later than 1992.

Index

bold figures indicate an illustration